D1577626

The Pocket Handbook of
Christian Living

Scripture Union
130 City Road, London EC1V 2NJ

Author: Derek Williams
Analysis and additional notes: Robert F. Hicks
Design: Fred Apps, Robert F. Hicks
Photography: Adrian Neilson, Robert F. Hicks, Alan Hayward, Robert Gainer Hunt, Peter Heaps, Paul Marsh

© Creative Publishing 1982
Ashwood House, 6 Pembroke Road, Moor Park,
Northwood, Middlesex, England.
UK Publisher 1982 Scripture Union
ISBN 0 86201 144 2

Biblical quotations are taken from the New International Version of the Bible.
© UK 1979 by the New York International Bible Society and used by permission.

Printed in Great Britain by Purnell and Sons (Book Production) Ltd., Paulton, Bristol

Arranged by Angus Hudson Ltd, London.

SECTION 9: ARRIVING

ON THE ROAD TO HEAVEN
Heaven on earth
Life in perspective
Aiming for goal
Ready for Jesus
Bible summary: Hope springs eternal

COPING WITH BEREAVEMENT
Coping with our grief
Coping with our loss
Coping, with Jesus' help
Helping others to cope
Bible summary: Why must we die?

FACING DEATH
Life completed
Saying goodbye
A place for repentance
The doorway to heaven
Bible summary: Life's last chance

ACTION REPLAY
Nothing is hidden
The fire test
Well done!
A place for you
Bible summary: The events of the end

WELCOME HOME!
A place of peace
A place of joy
A place of beauty
A place of justice
Bible summary: What happens to non-Christians?

LIFE'S NEW BEGINNING
All things new
A new body
A new understanding
A new kind of life
Bible summary: He is risen!

SECTION 8: SERVING

CALLED TO SERVE
Called by God
Compelled by love
Committed through faith
Concerned for others
Bible summary: Pictures of service

POWER TO SERVE
Sharing God's work
Filled with his Spirit
Controlled by his Word
Equipped with his gifts
Bible summary: Doing what comes naturally

SERVING IN THE CHURCH
The first shall be last
Lending a hand
Caring for the needy
Speaking God's word
Bible summary: Building community

INTO THE WORLD
A life that is different
Lips that are pure
Little things count
Loving our enemies
Bible summary: Pilgrims in a strange land

SHARING GOOD NEWS
A message for everyone
Talking about Jesus
Letting God work
Telling the neighbourhood
Bible summary: All things to all men

SERVICE FOR LIFE
Ready for change
Giving everything to Jesus
Supporting his workers
Praying for God's servants
Bible summary: Paul, a servant of God

SECTION 7: WINNING

JESUS IS KING
He conquered sin
He conquered death
He conquered evil
He will conquer the world
Bible summary: Jesus' cosmic plan

VICTORY IS CERTAIN
No need to sin
No need to fear
No need to doubt
No need to falter
Bible summary: He is able

RIGHT IN THE HEART
Jesus comes first
Thinking straight
Pure motives
Love determines action
Bible summary: Not I, but Christ

OVERCOMING EVIL
Be sure of your ground
Depend on God's power
Learning to say no
Tell Satan to go
Bible summary: The armour of God

RESISTING PRESSURE
The pressure to conform
The pressure to compromise
The pressure to complain
The pressure of complacency
Bible summary: United we stand

ONWARD CHRISTIAN SOLDIERS!
Building the kingdom
Salt in the world
Light for the world
Winning enemy territory
Bible summary: What is the kingdom of God?

SECTION 6: TESTING

THE REALITY OF TESTING
It happens to everyone
It may not seem fair
It is allowed by God
It can teach us more about God
Bible summary: The patience of Job

TESTING THROUGH DOUBT
A touch of humility
A touch of opposition
A touch of faith
A touch of confidence
Bible summary: The nature of faith

TESTING THROUGH TEMPTATIONS
An ever-present danger
Sometimes our own fault
Often subtle and cunning
Always a way out
Bible summary: Jesus' temptations

TESTING THROUGH FAILURE
The gospel for failures
The weakness of human nature
God's promise of success
The gospel of new beginnings
Bible summary: The disciple who failed Jesus

TESTING THROUGH PAIN
Pain in the world
Coping with suffering
Healing is possible
The end of all suffering
Bible summary: Paul's thorn in the flesh

TESTING THROUGH PERSECUTION
The gospel offends people
The ways they attack
The call to be faithful
Resisting, even to death
Bible summary: The promise of peace

SECTION 5: BELONGING

BELONGING TO GOD'S FAMILY
One Father
One Lord
One Spirit
One faith
Bible summary: All one in Christ

BELONGING TO EACH OTHER
Baptised into Christ
A club for sinners
A new set of friends
En route for heaven
Bible summary: A universal church

WORSHIPPING TOGETHER
The reason for worship
The object of worship
The source of worship
The value of worship
Bible summary: Make a joyful noise!

SHARING TOGETHER
Praying together
Learning together
Giving together
Eating together
Bible summary: One in fellowship

MINISTRIES FOR EACH OTHER
The need for leaders
The need for pastors and teachers
The need for organisers
The need for submission
Bible summary: Ministry in the New Testament

WORKING TOGETHER
The local church
A caring church
A witnessing church
A growing church
Bible summary: The church across the world

SECTION 4: DISCOVERING

DISCOVERING A NEW LIFE
Journey into life
A constant companion
New every morning
I know where I'm going
Bible summary: Becoming a disciple

DISCOVERING GOD'S WAY
Shown through conscience
Shown through God's law
Shown through Jesus
Shown through the Bible
Bible summary: The ten commandments

DISCOVERING GOD'S WILL
Praying it through
Searching the scriptures
Talking it over
Making up your mind
Bible summary: Living through faith

DISCOVERING GOD'S WORD
A book of truth
A book of example
A book of warning
A book of challenge
Bible summary: All we need to know

APPLYING GOD'S WORD
Equipment for the journey
A light for dark paths
A sword for hard battles
Strength to keep going
Bible summary: Jesus' view of the Bible

HANDLING GOD'S WORD
Reading it regularly
Soaking it up
Studying its teachings
Discovering its characters
Bible summary: Understanding God's Word

SECTION 3: GROWING

THE NEED FOR GROWTH
Growing into Christ
Growing in faith
Growing in knowledge
Growing in love
Bible summary: Becoming like Jesus

THE SOURCE OF GROWTH
The Spirit in us
The Spirit sanctifies us
The Spirit empowers us
The Spirit unites us
Bible summary: The fruit of the Spirit

THE EVIDENCE OF GROWTH
A growing experience
A growing confidence
A growing usefulness
A growing battle
Bible summary: The battle for the mind

THE SECRET OF GROWTH
In touch with God's purposes
Aware of God's presence
A source of God's power
Taking time to pray
Bible summary: What is prayer?

THE PATTERN FOR GROWTH
Love prayers
Sorry prayers
Thankyou prayers
Asking prayers
Bible summary: Jesus' pattern for prayer

THE PROBLEMS OF GROWTH
Exercising faith
Waiting for answers
Keeping alert
When God seems silent
Bible summary: God's mysterious ways

SECTION 2: KNOWING

KNOW YOURSELF
A spiritual person
A sinful person
A saved person
A separated person
Bible summary: A whole person

KNOWING GOD
A personal God
A holy God
A loving God
A purposeful God
Bible summary: Walking with God

KNOW YOUR ENEMY
The world
The flesh
The adversary
The last enemy
Bible summary: The devil still roars

KNOWING WHERE YOU STAND
Saved for ever
Kept from falling
Equipped for victory
Constantly forgiven
Bible summary: The unforgivable sin

KNOWING THE TRUTH
Set free by truth
Surrounded by truth
Taught by truth
Inspired by truth
Bible summary: Law and grace

KNOWING YOUR PRIVILEGES
Belonging to God's family
Being an ambassador
Bearing good news
Becoming a saint
Bible summary: Who is on the Lord's side?

SECTION 1: STARTING

WHAT IT'S ALL ABOUT
A life lived with God
A life given by God
A life dependent on God
A life lived for God
Bible Summary: What God has done

MAKING A NEW START
Seeing the need
Saying sorry to God
Saying no to sin
Saying yes to Jesus
Bible summary: What happens when you start

A NEW WAY OF LIVING
A new life
A new relationship
A new family
A new friend
Bible summary: The fullness of God

GOD'S UNBREAKABLE PROMISES
The promise of security
The promise of support
The promise of guidance
The promise of his presence
Bible summary: God keeps his word

THE HELP WHICH GOD GIVES
Help through prayer
Help through the Bible
Help from God's people
Help through worship
Bible summary: Everyone has needs

A PERMANENT LIFE
A joyful life
A growing life
A giving life
An everlasting life
Bible summary: How perfect can you get?

USE IT IN A CHURCH PROGRAMME

Ministers, pastors and teachers will find this handbook an invaluable reference manual for subject material when preparing programmes for the church. The material could be used by taking, for example, the six studies as the basis for a six-week course of Sunday sermons or mid-week meetings.

The headings throughout the book are designed to capture the truth of the Bible. It is hoped that this will be helpful to preachers and teachers alike.

USE IT IN SCHOOLS AND COLLEGES

The teaching matter, scripture passages and questions will help to stimulate those involved in religious education, as well as members of informal religious discussion groups and forums. The handbook has been planned as a comprehensive aid so that students from many different backgrounds of worship and tradition may learn together from the Bible's teaching in a way that prepares them for life.

'It gives me great pleasure to recommend **The Handbook of Christian Living**, the companion to **The Handbook of Christian Truth**. Just as it is important that Christians *know* what they *believe*, equally it is important that they *practise* what they *know*. This fresh and compelling series will be a real help in putting many Christians on the right track and keeping them going in the right direction.'

Richard Bewes

HOW TO USE THIS BOOK

Used rightly, this handbook should give years of valuable service in a number of ways. The material has been arranged for the maximum flexibility of use, and for a wide range of situations and readers.

USE IT IN PERSONAL STUDY

This handbook is a companion to the Bible. It may be used as a reference book to the teaching of the Bible, but it may also be used for personal, regular study of the scriptures. The book is made up of fifty-four studies, and if one main section is studied each week, the total material will be covered in the course of a year.

By using a good reference Bible or concordance, each study may be extended. The passages given in the Bible Check can serve as a starting-point for the reader to do his own discovering in the Bible. In this way a comprehensive view of each theme can be built up. It would be useful for you to have your own notebook alongside the handbook.

USE IT IN A GROUP

The material in this handbook will be of particular value in the ever-increasing number of house-groups, where Christian people meet together. Study groups of all ages will greatly profit from the teaching they will discover for themselves as they follow the guide-lines given in the book. It will also prove beneficial to women's groups, especially where new-comers to the Christian faith are eager to learn the practical implications of their belief.

We would encourage group leaders to make the following preparations before using the handbook in any discussion. First, they should become familiar with the Bible passages provided, and be prepared to support these with cross-references. Second, they should carefully read through the study material itself. Third, they should be prepared to use the questions as a basis for discussion, and to prepare further questions of their own.

Some extra features about this handbook are:

1 Each study has four divisions which help in retaining the key truths presented.

2 Key Bible passages and references are also provided with every study so that you can see what God's word actually says about it.

3 Included in every study are questions ('Something to think about'). We trust this will be a real help, especially when used in groups.

4 Each main study is introduced with a 'Key truth' and concluded with a 'Postcript'. Again, this has been provided to help you to retain important truths.

5 Beside the 54 main studies we have added 'Bible summaries'. Each 'Bible summary' follows a main study and is complete in itself. We would encourage you to supplement the main study by looking up the references and Bible passages in the 'Bible summary'.

6 The pictures selected separate the 54 studies. They also enhance the teaching in the 'Bible summary'. The comments to the pictures have been added as a connecting link.

7 There is one thing that we have not provided and that is the help of the Spirit of God to all those who seek to live for him. We do with confidence, however, commend to you a dependence on him as you seek to understand the Christian life, in order to live and make progress as a Christian.

This handbook is now yours. The Christian life for all of us is a matter of progress, and each day brings new opportunities for growth. It is the sincere prayer of all those who have been involved in bringing this handbook to you that you will find it a useful guide in living the Christian life.

Derek Williams
Robert F. Hicks

FOREWORD

This handbook is for all those who not only want to 'understand' but also to 'live' to their fullest capacity the Christian life.

At first you may think that everybody who claims to be a Christian will want to be a 'Jesus person' and follow him. Unfortunately this is not the case.

Most people support a particular sport or group but how many people actually participate? This 'Handbook of Christian Living' is for participators, for all those who really want to be involved and make progress in the Christian life.

To be a 'participator' we have to start, and the best place to start is at the beginning! But starting at the beginning does not mean stopping there. We must move on if we are going to know the real thrill of participating in this adventure with God.

Obviously we shall make many mistakes as we progress. Indeed, the mistakes we make will in themselves encourage us to depend more on God, realising that he is only too willing to help us. Real, lasting progress is always the result of this partnership with God.

This book itself is like a journey. Starting with the first section, we move on through the nine main areas of practical Christian living until we come to the final section, entitled Arriving.

The nine main sections are as follows:

STARTING	**KNOWING**	**GROWING**
DISCOVERING	**BELONGING**	**TESTING**
WINNING	**SERVING**	**ARRIVING**

These nine main sections each have six complete studies, giving to the individual or group fifty-four studies in all.

INTRODUCTION

Years ago, when I first became a Christian, I was given a simple handbook full of helpful Christian teaching, together with Bible verses so that I could check up on them for myself. It was published by Scripture Union. This new volume of Bible studies for the individual reader or for groups gives an up-to-date version of that same idea, also published by Scripture Union.

However, books look much more attractive nowadays than they did then! The two-page layout with questions to think about, followed by a Bible survey, is, I believe, a helpful method of study.

It is so important that we do use the Bible checks. It is easy just to imitate what other Christians do, without asking first whether this is actually what God himself has commanded and what his Son taught. The Holy Spirit is the Author of Scripture, who moved the human writers, and therefore we need to submit ourselves to God's authority in the written Word.

I am glad, too, that the first volume – THE HANDBOOK OF CHRISTIAN TRUTH – is now to be joined by this volume, THE HANDBOOK OF CHRISTIAN LIVING. Christian belief must produce beautiful behaviour. A correct understanding of truth must be backed up by a convincing demonstration of Christian living. Sceptical people will not come to share our belief in the Lord Jesus unless they see beautiful lives, as we 'walk as Jesus did.'

So, whether you use this in a small group or use it alongside an open Bible morning or evening, I hope that you will work through it carefully, that it will be a blessing to you personally and to all who see us living Christian lives.

Dr Michael Griffiths,
Principal,
London Bible College.

Starting

If you decide to read and think about this book, it suggests that you have the most important quality for starting the Christian life – *desire*. Desire, of course, may be reflected in different ways. There is the . . .

Desire to know what Christianity is
Desire to have what Christians possess
Desire for fulfilment in personal life
Desire for peace of mind when worried.

Whatever the reason, this first of nine studies will help you to *know*, *seek*, *discover* and by faith *experience*, the reality of being a Christian.

THE MATTERHORN (Adrian Neilson)

WHAT IT'S ALL ABOUT

The key truth: *Being a Christian consists of a close personal relationship with God, and not just of following a certain code of behaviour.*

A life lived with God

Many people think that being a Christian is a matter of living in a certain way: being kind to others, giving to charities, going to church services, and not committing crimes or frauds.

The Bible sees it differently, however. While all these things are part of living a Christian life, the essence is called 'faith'. That means trusting God personally, as well as believing certain truths.

Jesus complained that some of the religious people of his day had become so tied up by rules and regulations that they were neglecting their relationship with God. The gospel, or good news, is that ordinary people can once again know God personally and live in harmony with him.

To think about *Why do some people try to turn a simple relationship with God into a system of rules?*

A life given by God

Since the world began, people have tried to find God. They have invented all kinds of ways to please him. But the whole Bible shows how futile these attempts are. Because people have refused to obey God's commands, the whole world is now cut off from him.

The only way a person can make lasting contact with God is to welcome Jesus into his life. He was God's perfect Son, who became a man in order to explain God's purposes to the world. And when he died, he took on himself the punishment for man's rebellion, and opened up the way for us to God.

BIBLE CHECK
A life lived with God: John 17:3; 2 Timothy 1:12

No one can create a new relationship with God for himself. He has already done everything necessary; his way can only be accepted – or rejected.

To think about *List some of the ways people use to try to reach God; why are they never good enough?*

A life dependent on God

Trusting Jesus is not like wearing a lucky charm. It is not simply a way of getting on the right side of God and making sure of a place in heaven.

Being a Christian is a matter of trusting God all the time. It involves staying in touch with him so that we receive his instructions and do what he asks each day.

It can bring a whole new dimension to our lives. But the Christian life will not always be easy. Saying 'no' to wrong things is often difficult. Facing unexpected problems can be shattering. But he promises to help all who follow him.

To think about *Depending on God may mean giving up our own selfishness or pride. But why does it make sense to do so?*

A life lived for God

Most important of all, being a Christian means living **for** God. Some people throw everything into work, family life, or special interests. The Christian is called to put all his energy into serving and pleasing God.

That does not mean that he is expected to stop what he is doing and become a preacher or a missionary! Each person has talents and abilities which God wants to be fully used, with love and care. He wants a person's faith to influence all his relationships and activities.

The Bible never separates 'believing' from 'doing'. Faith and work go together. If you emphasise one more than the other, you may have a philosophy or a lifestyle, but you will not have true Christianity.

To think about *If God has loved us so much, how should we regard other people?*

A life given by God: John 14:6; Acts 4:12
A life dependent on God: Luke 9:23–25; John 15:1–5
A life lived for God: Matthew 6:24; James 2:14–18

BIBLE SUMMARY

What God has done

The Bible describes how the first people who knew God refused to do what he asked. Ever since, mankind has been disobeying God's laws. So people are out of touch with God in this life, and prevented by death from enjoying eternal life in heaven (Ephesians 2:1–3).

A picture of hope

The Old Testament tells how God showed people how they could get in touch with him again. He told them to obey his laws. And he said that their sin was so serious that the only remedy for it was an innocent victim – an animal in those days – who would carry the death penalty on their behalf (Leviticus 16:6–10).

But that was only a picture of God's greatest act of love. Animals could not provide a permanent solution. The New Testament says: 'God so loved the world that he gave his one and only Son, that whoever believes in him shall not perish but have eternal life' (John 3:16).

An act of love

Jesus Christ was the only sinless person who has ever lived. Even his enemies could not fault him. And he saw his death as 'a ransom for many' (Mark 10:45); the innocent suffered the sentence passed on the guilty. John the Baptist called him, 'The Lamb of God, who takes away the sin of the world' (John 1:29).

But because he was God as well as man, he conquered death by rising to life again, and promised that all who welcomed him would receive eternal life (John 3:36).

That life was to begin at once. It is knowing God for oneself, and enjoying his presence for ever (Romans 8:38,39).

For thought and prayer *God is good and great; we are sinful and weak. God had no need to save us from our sins; he did so because he loved us. 'Thank you, Lord!'*

SIGNPOST AT TOP OF SNOWBALL MOUNTAIN, USA (Robert F. Hicks)

The Old Testament is full of signs and promises, pointing to the time when God's Son would come, live among us, die for us, then rise victorious over death and sin.

MAKING A NEW START

The key truth *Becoming a Christian is like starting life all over again, by handing over the control of our lives to Jesus Christ.*

Seeing the need

God is a person almost beyond our imagination. He is the powerful creator of everything which exists, yet he also knows just how each individual thinks and feels. He is holy, too – he can do nothing wrong.

By contrast, none of us is perfect. We have not always kept God's laws. We have done things which even our conscience knows are wrong. And above all, we have left God out of our thinking.

As a result, we are separated from God by a barrier largely of our own construction: self-will, self-indulgence and self-confidence. The Bible calls this barrier sin. It prevents us from knowing God personally.

To think about *What is the root cause of all human sinfulness?*

Saying sorry to God

None of us like to admit that we have been wrong. It is even harder if we have to admit that the whole direction of our life so far has been off-course – going our way instead of God's.

But we cannot get to know God for ourselves without first telling him we are sorry for having neglected him and for the wrong things we have done. And that includes thoughts and words as well as actions.

Perhaps we also need to say sorry to other people whom we have hurt along the way.

To think about *Why do we need to say sorry to God for things which have offended other people?*

Saying no to sin

We often teach children to say sorry when they do

BIBLE CHECK

Seeing the need: 1 John 1:5–8; Romans 6:23

wrong, but watch them blunder on in the same way moments afterwards! **Saying** sorry is not enough; we have to **show** we mean it, too.

God knows what we are really like, and words never fool him. We must put all our sin behind us, and promise him not to go wilfully our own way again. This is what the Bible calls 'repentance'.

For some people this may involve a very radical change in the way they live. For others the change will be more inward, in the way they think and speak. God promises to help us, whatever is involved.

To think about *The Bible talks about the pleasures of sin. But what does God offer to those who are determined to live for him?*

Saying yes to Jesus

Jesus has already done everything necessary to restore our relationship with God by dying on the cross and rising from the dead. He offers the gift of 'eternal life' to anyone who will accept it.

But we cannot be half-hearted about it; we cannot ask God for his forgiveness if we are not also prepared to let him take charge of our life from then on.

If you have never made a fresh start with Jesus, or if your Christian life has become stuck in a rut, you can use a simple prayer like this: 'Dear God, I am sorry I have left you out of my life, and sinned against you in thought, word and deed. Thank you for sending Jesus to die on the cross so that I could know you for myself. Forgive my sin, and give me the power of your Spirit to live for you every day until you bring me to be with you for ever in heaven. For Jesus' sake, Amen.'

To think about *Being a Christian is living a 'new' life: what is new about it?*

Postscript *Jesus called people to follow him just as they were, without trying to reform themselves first. But he also said that once they had begun to follow him, he would change them himself.*

Saying sorry to God: 1 John 1:9,10; Psalm 51: 1–4,10–12
Saying no to sin: Matthew 4:17; Ephesians 4:22–24
Saying yes to Jesus: Revelation 3:20; Matthew 11:28–30

BIBLE SUMMARY

What happens when you start

There are a number of pictures in the Bible which illustrate what happens when a person welcomes Jesus into his life. Three of them have one thing in common: they refer to a family. (see Ephésians 2:19.)

A happy event

The first picture is of a baby born into the family. When a person accepts Jesus as the one who has cleared away his sin and opened up the way to God, he is 'born again' (John 3:3). He has become a true child of God, because God's Spirit has given him a new, eternal life (John 1:12,13). And like a new human baby, the new Christian has a lot of learning to do, and he can easily make mistakes or even be led astray (1 Peter 2:1,2).

A new status

The next picture is that of adoption, when a child of one family is accepted as a true son or daughter of another. No one has the right to belong to God's family. Everyone is by nature shut out of it; they belong to the devil's domain. But God adopts those who trust Jesus into his family, welcoming them as his own children (Romans 8:15,16).

Where we belong

Finally, there is the well-known picture of 'coming home'. In Jesus' parable of the lost son, a rebellious child decides to come home, sorry for having run away, wasted his life and brought shame on the family (Luke 15:11–32). His father, God, sees him from a distance, goes out to meet him, and welcomes him home. His sin is forgiven, and the family celebrates his return.

For thought and prayer *Which of these pictures most closely reflects your experience? Thank God for what he has done for you.*

MOTHER WITH HER NEW-BORN CHILD
(Adrian Neilson)
*The new birth shows us the **experience** of salvation. Being adopted shows us the **state** and **privilege** of belonging to God. Coming home shows us the need for a **personal response**.*

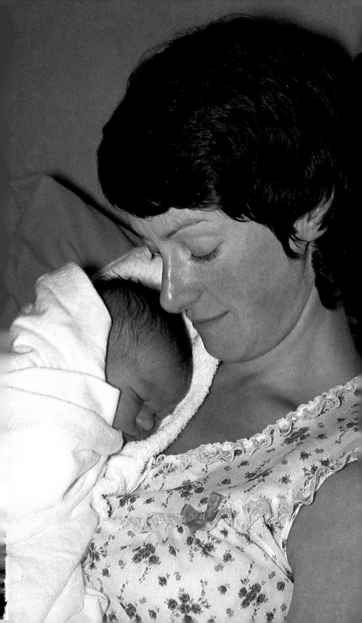

A NEW WAY OF LIVING

The key truth *Living as a Christian means enjoying and experiencing life in a totally new way.*

A new life

Before Jesus Christ enters our lives we are spiritually dead – unable to know God and draw on his help. But once we have committed ourselves to him, he promises to make everything fresh and new.

He gives a new quality of life which is open to God and lasts for ever. It includes new hope, peace and joy, and power and patience to cope with difficulties.

It has new standards of conduct, and new attitudes, too. But all these things are given to us by God, and cannot be created by our own efforts.

To think about *God's help to us is 'new every morning'; how can we keep our experience of him fresh?*

A new relationship

To the Christian, God is no longer a distant, shadowy figure. He is a real person who can be known, loved and worshipped.

He is like a new friend, always ready to help and strengthen us. But the Bible usually calls him 'Father', because like the best human fathers he promises to provide all we need to carry out his purposes.

Sometimes he will tell us off. But he never bullies his children. And for our part, it will take time to get to know him better.

To think about *List all the qualities you think an ideal father should have: God has them all!*

BIBLE CHECK
A new life: 2 Corinthians 5:17,18; Colossians 3:12–17

A new family

If the Christian were an only child of our heavenly Father, life would be very lonely. But in fact we are born into the worldwide family of God. In every town and district we have 'brothers and sisters' who love the Father.

This family is usually called the church. It may be large or small in a local situation, and like human families it is not always perfect. But it has important functions.

It exists to help each Christian grow in the faith. God has provided it so that we can find the support and encouragement we need.

To think about *Some people try to go it alone as Christians; what are they likely to miss?*

A new friend

When Jesus was on earth, his followers were upset when he spoke of leaving them. But he promised to send 'The Comforter', the Holy Spirit, to be with them.

The Holy Spirit is God active in the Christian's life. He points us to Jesus, helps us understand the Bible and speak to God in prayer. He shows up what is wrong in our lives, and gives power to put it right.

And he promises to give us abilities to help other Christians, using God's strength, not our own.

To think about *We need spiritual help to live a spiritual life: to what extent are you drawing on that help?*

Postscript *The new life is a gift from God. Some people only allow him to make superficial changes to their lives, but Jesus wants to change us right through.*

A new relationship: John 14:23; 1 Peter 5:7
A new family: 1 Peter 2:9,10; Ephesians 2:19–22
A new friend: John 14:26; 1 Corinthians 12:4–11

BIBLE SUMMARY

The fullness of God

When we describe what God does for us, we use different names for him: Father, Son (Jesus), and Holy Spirit. Sometimes people mistakenly think they are different gods, or that only one has any relevance to us today.

In fact, God reveals himself as three 'persons'. Each is fully God, but also has a different function. But when we talk about God being 'in' a Christian's life, all three persons are involved (John 14:23).

Christ in you

Jesus, the Son of God, lives in us from the moment we receive him as the one who takes away our sin and gives us eternal life (Colossians 1:27). He promises never to leave us (Hebrews 13:5).

Filled with the Spirit

The Holy Spirit also enters our life at the same time (Ephesians 1:13,14). But the Bible also speaks of other times during the Christian life when he 'fills' a person, usually when they face a special task (e.g. Acts 4:31). However, we should always be filled with the Spirit, his life flowing into and out of us to others (Ephesians 5:18).

When we specially need the Spirit's blessing to help us worship or serve God, Jesus tells us to ask the Father and we will be given the power of the Holy Spirit (Luke 11:13).

But he never gives his power in advance of its being used. And there are times when he cannot fill us, because sin has crowded him out (Ephesians 4:30).

For thought and prayer *To know the continuous fullness of God, we must go on being surrendered to him. What does this imply for your experience today?*

KRIMML FALLS, AUSTRIA (Adrian Neilson)
Rivers of life. One of the wonders of the Christian experience is that God is willing to come into our lives by his Holy Spirit. This is not only to fill us with himself, but also through us to come to others.

GOD'S UNBREAKABLE PROMISES

The key truth *God promises to help us in many ways, and he never breaks his word.*

The promise of security

We do not know what will happen tomorrow. We may face entirely new circumstances: poverty or wealth; illness or tragedy; hard decisions, unexpected opportunities, changes in relationships.

Because life is to some extent uncertain, we are often tempted to find a sense of security in familiar objects or people. But they can change too. Only God offers perfect security.

He promises never to let go of his children. He will never abandon us even if we forget him. He holds us secure in his love all through this life, and into the next.
To think about *Imagine how you would feel if, having let someone down, he still trusts and loves you. What does this teach you about God's love for you?*

The promise of support

We are most conscious of the need for God's help when we face difficulty or temptation. But if we are to do everything God wants, we need to draw on his power all the time.

In fact, we need his support just as much when life is running smoothly. Then it is easy to forget him, and so to fail him by something we do or say.

God promises his help at all times. But he never promises to brush aside our problems. Problems, in fact, often become opportunities to experience and demonstrate his power.

BIBLE CHECK
The promise of security: John 6:37–39; Romans 8:38,39
The promise of support: Matthew 11:28–30; Philippians

To think about *What reasons can you think of which explain why the Christian needs to depend on God's help for even the smallest of tasks?*

The promise of guidance

For many people, the journey through life is rather like stumbling through a dark forest. It is hard to find the way which will be most rewarding.

God, because he knows both us and the circumstances of our life in every detail, promises to show us the right thing to do at each step along the way.

He has a special purpose for each person, too, and he promises to lead us to it. So as we go in the direction he has prepared, we experience our new harmony with him.

To think about *Why does it make good sense to give God a free hand in planning your life?*

The promise of his presence

Sometimes Christians complain that life for the very first followers of Jesus must have been much easier than it is now, because they could see and touch their master.

But, in fact, it was harder. Jesus could only be in one place at a time. Now he promises to be with everyone, everywhere, who loves and serves him.

We may not always feel him near us, but the Bible is never in any doubt. Jesus said, 'I will be with you always, to the very end of the age' (Matthew 28:20). He is always on hand to help, teach and guide us.

To think about *Although Jesus is the Son of God, he is also called our friend. Think about the qualities of his friendship.*

Postscript *Human beings often break the promises they make because they are weak and imperfect; God can never break his because he is all-powerful and perfect.*

4:11–13
The promise of guidance: Psalm 32:8; Isaiah 30:21
The promise of his presence: Psalm 139:7–12; Matthew 28:19,20

BIBLE SUMMARY

God keeps his word

Some people will promise anything, but never do what they say. God is not like that. He cannot change his mind and let us down. In the Old Testament he was specially known as a God who made solemn promises (or 'covenants') and kept his word (Deuteronomy 7:9).

Two-edged promises

But as the nation of Israel soon found out, God's promises are two-edged. We can only enjoy all that he offers if we continue to obey him (Deuteronomy 7:10,11). Some of his promises, of course, are unaffected by human sin. He does not rob Christians of eternal life when they do not obey him (John 6:39).

That truth is, however, intended to inspire us to loving devotion, and not encourage us to be careless. God is so gracious that he loves us even when we ignore him (Romans 6:1–4).

Three special promises

The Bible stresses three special promises of God. He promised Noah that he would never again destroy the earth by flood in his anger at human sin (Genesis 9:15).

He promised that Abraham would be the father of many nations, and have a special close relationship with God. And in believing that promise Abraham demonstrated what faith really is (Genesis 17:7,8).

And he made a 'new covenant' with the Christian church through the death of Jesus; that he would be our God and we would be his people for ever (Hebrews 8:6–13).

For thought and prayer *If God keeps his promises, what should be our attitude to them?*

A RAINBOW (Alan Hayward)
The rainbow is a continual reminder that God keeps his word. Christian assurance grows as we accept God's promises.

THE HELP WHICH GOD GIVES

The key truth *God has provided four special ways in which we can receive his help.*

Help through prayer

We often have lots of questions to ask God. Prayer is the way in which we can tell him how we feel, what our needs are, and share with him the problems and opportunities we face.

The Bible tells us that God is always ready to listen to our prayers, and loves to answer them. But sometimes we ask for things which will take us away from his purposes, so he will not give us these. We may be so full of requests that we never stop to ask what he really wants.

And he frequently waits for us to ask before giving us what we need, because only when we ask humbly are we ready to receive gratefully.

To think about *'God is always more willing to give than we are to ask'.* Why?

Help through the Bible

Our relationship with God is always two-way. We talk to him in prayer, and one of his methods of speaking to us is through the Bible, which is sometimes called his 'Word'.

The Bible authors were guided by God as they wrote down their experiences of him and the truths he revealed. All God wants us to know about himself and how to live for him are contained in its pages.

And the Holy Spirit will make it come alive to us and apply it to our circumstances, if we seek his insight.

To think about *Jesus relied heavily on the Bible of his day (the Old Testament). Why should we rely on the Bible?*

BIBLE CHECK
Help through prayer: John 16:24; Matthew 7:7–11
Help through the Bible: 2 Timothy 3:16,17; John 16:12–15

Help from God's people

We have already seen that God has made us members of his family. Our 'brothers and sisters' in Christ have special gifts and insights which God uses to help us. In fact, he intends that we should be almost as dependent on each other as on him, for we all lack wisdom.

Some people will be able to help us understand God's truth and the Bible better. Others will be able to advise us about our problems. We can talk and pray with them, and learn together from the Bible, sharing with all what God shows to each.

And it is always a good idea to talk to other Christians before making important decisions, to receive both advice and support.

To think about *Some Christians want to go it alone and never receive help from other people. How would you explain that this is not a good idea?*

Help through worship

Worship happens when a group of Christians meet together to express love and gratitude to God for all that he is and all he has done. They may sing and even shout; they may be quiet and thoughtful. And, of course, we can worship God on our own, as we think about his love to us.

Praising God helps us in two ways. First, it reminds us of how great he is. The things which concern us then seem smaller, and our confidence grows in God's ability to deal with them.

And secondly, it opens us to the Holy Spirit, making us more able to hear and obey him, and to receive his power.

To think about *Paul and Silas sang hymns when shut in a filthy prison (Acts 16:25). Why can we worship God even when life seems very hard?*

Postscript *Make a list of all the things you could praise God for; then praise him!*

Help from God's people: Ephesians 4:11–14; Romans 12:4–8
Help through worship: Acts 4:31; Psalm 29:1–4,10,11

BIBLE SUMMARY

Everyone has needs

Even Jesus himself, his closest followers and all the great characters of the Bible, needed to use prayer, the Scriptures, 'fellowship' with God's people, and worship, to keep themselves in harmony with God.

Prayer often preceded important events. Jesus prayed all night before choosing his twelve apostles (Luke 6:12,13). And they and their close friends 'devoted themselves' to prayer after Jesus left the earth, before the Holy Spirit filled them with power on the Day of Pentecost (Acts 1:14).

A weapon for battle

Jesus used the Scriptures as a weapon to fight off the subtle and powerful temptations he received in the desert before he began his public ministry (Matthew 4:3–11). The Psalmist said that the way to lead a pure life was to store God's Word in his memory so that he could draw on it at a moment's notice (Psalm 119:11).

Caring for each other

Paul often writes appreciatively of the help he was given by other Christians (e.g. Colossians 4:7–11). The Bible records the ways in which God's people cared for each other. It was a care which sometimes meant rebuking and challenging, as well as encouraging, each other.

As for worship, it seems to have been such a natural desire and thing to do (e.g. Acts 20:7) that only in extreme cases is it actually commanded (Hebrews 10:24,25).

For thought and prayer *The helps which God gives take time to use. What steps do we need to take to ensure we have enough time for them?*

SUNSET OVER A HOUSE (Robert F. Hicks)
Throughout the history of Christianity the home has played an important part in helping many to experience God's truth and love.

A PERMANENT LIFE

The key truth *The Christian life never stops; there is always more to learn, and heaven to look forward to.*

A joyful life

Jesus promised his followers the two things which everyone wants but few ever find; inner peace and joy. Neither depend on an easy life. Rather, they stem from the confidence that our loving Father is in control of it, whatever happens.

Christian joy is a sense of thankfulness for God's care and love. We are no longer tied down by our sin but are free to be the people he intended us to be. We really have something to celebrate!

Joy is a gift from God, however, and not something we can just turn on or manufacture by a certain technique. And it always focuses on him, and is not a feeling to be enjoyed for its own sake.

To think about *Jesus promised a depth of peace which the world cannot give; how does it differ from ordinary experience?*

A growing life

The Christian life has only just begun when a person becomes a member of God's new family. Just as a human child has many things to learn, and takes a long time over it, so too does a child of God.

There is always something new to learn about God and his ways. And Scripture tells us to go on to perfection – which is a long way ahead! Growing in faith can be an exciting, as well as an exacting, adventure.

Sometimes we will only grow more like Jesus when we face difficulty and apply our faith to it, just as he did. But he also promises to renew our old, sinful nature, so that we steadily move forward in our Christian lives.

BIBLE CHECK
A joyful life: John 15:11; Psalm 95:1–7

To think about *A mature person is always willing to learn. Discuss things you have learnt recently – and the things you know you need to learn!*

A giving life

Christian faith is not meant to be kept to ourselves. The first followers of Jesus couldn't stop telling others of what God had done for them.

We have something to give to the world – a 'gospel', or 'good news', which transforms people's lives, attitudes and relationships.

And we have something to share with each other, too: love and concern, some new gift or ability, a possession – anything which will help build up others' faith and minister to their needs. Only as we give in faith will we grow in it.

To think about *Most people put their own interests before those of other people. Why is this not a Christian attitude?*

An everlasting life

Some Christians are laughed at as being 'too heavenly minded to be of any earthly use'. We are not meant to be useless. Our ultimate home is heaven, but our feet are to be firmly on the ground.

But, in fact, sometimes we may not be heavenly minded enough. We have been promised eternal life in heaven with Jesus for ever. That is meant to inspire and encourage us in our life now.

We know that death is not the end for us. We have nothing to fear for the future. We have hope, and we shall not be disappointed in the wonderful place God has waiting for us.

To think about *Many people regard a place in heaven as their right. What does the Bible say about who will be there?*

Postscript *Jesus said that the Christian life is a narrow path, compared to the broad road of self-indulgence followed by many other people. But his way leads to abundant life now and for ever.*

A growing life: Philippians 3:12–16; Ephesians 4:13,14
A giving life: John 13:34,35; Luke 6:38
An everlasting life: Revelation 22:1–5; Philippians 1:21–24

BIBLE SUMMARY

How perfect can you get?

Jesus told his followers that they should be 'perfect', or mature Christians (Matthew 5:48). Although God's Word promises forgiveness for the sins a Christian commits, it does not expect him unconcernedly to commit them (1 John 2:1,2). Jesus himself was perfect, and we are to follow his example (1 Peter 2:21–23).

But we are not instantly made perfect when we receive Jesus, even though our sin is swept away and is no longer a barrier between us and God. His life enters us, his power is available to us, and we have to learn to make use of it. This takes time, and we will make mistakes (James 3:1,2).

Becoming perfect

The Bible tells us to become perfect by obeying God's will (1 Peter 1:14–16). As we do so, we become more skilled in understanding and knowing what God wants us to do (Hebrews 5:12–14).

Sometimes we will get frustrated, because our own human nature, which still retains its imperfections and limitations, never quite manages to be as good or do as well as God's Spirit within us is urging us to. There is a battle going on inside us between the old and the new (Romans 7:15–25).

Battling against evil

And there is a battle against evil, too, as we are tempted, mocked and unsettled by evil forces which come sometimes from the most surprising quarters (Ephesians 6:12,13). But Jesus' people are promised victory over them (1 John 5:4,5).

For thought and prayer *There is no room for complacency in the Christian life. How can we make sure we are still pressing on to know Jesus better?*

Knowing

The Christian faith is not blind faith; we know why, what and whom we believe. God gives to all believers understanding and a special wisdom that the world does not possess. As we are prepared to use our hearts and minds, God will give us the teaching help of his Holy Spirit in understanding . . .

The uniqueness of ourselves
The reality of God
The dangers from our enemies
The assurance of faith
The freedom of truth
The value of our privileges.

SEEING AND REFLECTING THE MATTERHORN
(Adrian Neilson)

KNOW YOURSELF

The key truth *We can only fully appreciate all that Jesus has done for us when we see ourselves as he sees us.*

A spiritual person

God has made every human being a unique person. But we all have certain things in common, such as a similar physical shape, and such abilities as speech, thought and emotion.

We also have a natural desire to seek God. Unlike other creatures, we can know him in a personal way, although many people have a substitute 'god' which they devote their lives to.

God gave us this ability so that we would live in harmony with him. Lives which include worship and love of God through Jesus Christ start to become what God intended they should be.

To think about *List the various 'substitute gods' people have invented. Why is serving Jesus better than them all?*

A sinful person

Nobody except Jesus himself has lived a fully perfect life. It was because of people's failure to obey God's laws (our 'sinfulness') that Jesus had to die on the cross.

But even the Christian, who has accepted Jesus' death on his behalf as the way to knowing God, remains sinful. Every part of us is still less than perfect – our thoughts, knowledge and actions.

That is why sometimes we fail to live the Christian life as fully as we intend. It is still easy to fall into the old ways of living. But Jesus always gives us his power to avoid sinning if we ask for it.

To think about *Why should a Christian avoid sinning?*

BIBLE CHECK
A spiritual person: Acts 17:26,27; Philippians 2:9–11

A saved person

Christians often talk about being 'saved from their sins'. To some people that sounds like the language of another culture. But everyone knows people are saved from burning houses, or from drowning in rivers.

So a Christian is a person who has been saved from a terrible fate – living without God for ever. And we are 'saved' the moment we receive Jesus into our lives, just as a drowning person is saved the moment he is grabbed by his rescuer.

But being saved is not just a past experience. Having been saved is a constant fact and continuous experience; we have been given a new life.

To think about *Imagine what it must be like to be saved from certain death. In what ways is your experience of Jesus like that?*

A separated person

Jesus has called us to set aside the ways of the world. This does not mean going into seclusion, but abandoning the attitudes to life and other people which are common in our society when these conflict with Jesus' love and purposes.

Sometimes that will mean saying 'no' to things we used to like or enjoy, because they will hinder our relationship with him.

But more important, it means saying 'yes' to what he wants. When the Bible uses the word 'holy', it means being dedicated to doing God's will. It involves caring for others, sharing Jesus' love, and avoiding sin.

To think about *What Christian attitudes can you think of which are not usually shared by non-Christians?*

Postscript *While we all have certain characteristics in common, God made us with quite different personalities. We are not meant to look or feel the same, nor to do the same things as others, and he deals with us just as we are.*

A sinful person: Romans 3:23; 1 John 2:1,2
A saved person: 1 Timothy 1:15; Matthew 1:21
A separated person: Matthew 6:24; Ephesians 2:8–10

BIBLE SUMMARY

A whole person

Sometimes people talk about parts of the human personality as if they were all quite separate. They speak as if the body had a mind of its own! Although the Bible does distinguish between different parts, it never regards them as separate. When it refers to one part, it intends us to see the whole person from that angle.

The mind or heart

'Mind' and 'heart' often mean the same in scripture. They refer to a person as a thinking, feeling being. Emotion is part of the Christian's life (Romans 12:15). Even Jesus wept (John 11:35,36). But God gave us minds so that our reactions would always be based on an understanding of God's truth (Romans 12:2).

The body

The Bible never regards the body or its functions as sinful, even though sinful things are done with it (Romans 12:1). It is to be cared for (1 Corinthians 6:19,20). After death we will be raised to life by God who will then give us a new body which will never decay or grow old (1 Corinthians 15:42–44).

Soul and spirit

The 'soul' refers to the whole living person. The word is often translated as 'life' (Mark 8:35,36). Often soul and spirit are used interchangeably. Spirit, however, sometimes has a more precise meaning. It can refer to our inner motives. So the Egyptian king who refused to let Moses leave his country was hardened in spirit (Exodus 7:14). And when Paul prayed with his spirit (1 Corinthians 14:14) as well as with his mind, his whole being was involved in that prayer.

To think and pray about *Psalm 8 says God has made people 'a little lower than the angels': think what this means and praise God for it.*

ENJOYING LIFE AS A FAMILY (Adrian Nielson)
The more complete (whole) we are as people, the more satisfying life will be. Supremely the mission of Jesus Christ is to make people whole.

KNOWING GOD

The key truth *God is a person with whom we can have a lasting, growing relationship of love and trust.*

A personal God

All through the Bible, God is thought of as a person. He is never regarded merely as a force or power, like electricity, which only works in set ways.

Of course, he is not entirely like a human person. He does not forget his promises, he never stops loving, and he does not lose his temper!

But he is *personal*. The Bible has many accounts of how he spoke to people, showed them his plans, and taught them how to respond to him. Its central message is that he can be known by anyone at any time and in any place.

To think about *What steps can you take in order to get to know God better?*

A holy God

Although God loves and cares, there is another side to his character. He can do nothing wrong himself, and he cannot accept wrong-doing by others.

He is often described as holy. That means he is perfect in himself, and separated from all that is imperfect. That is why Jesus had to die on the cross: the perfect man suffered the just punishment for our sins so that we could know this holy God.

Each time a Christian does something which is against God's holiness, the relationship with him is hurt, although not destroyed – just as when a close friend lets down the person he loves.

To think about *How should God's holiness affect our daily lives?*

BIBLE CHECK
A personal God: John 17:3; 2 Timothy 1:12
A holy God: 1 Peter 1:14–16; Leviticus 11:44,45; Isaiah

A loving God

God's love is so much greater than human love because it continues when it is not deserved, or even rejected. And because it is a pure, holy love, it does not depend on what we are like, nor does it spring from favouritism.

The Christian encounters God's love first at the cross. In his love for us, God sent his Son to live and die in the world.

But we can experience it every day, too, as we ask for and receive his help and guidance, as we discover his power, and as we see all he has done. Even in the darkest times, his love still shines through.

To think about *If God loves us so much, how would he expect us to regard other people?*

A purposeful God

The world is very old, and there have been many generations of people living in it. God, who created it, has long-term plans which he has worked out over many centuries.

The best example is the long time he took preparing the Jewish nation for the birth of Jesus. For us, it means we live at a point in history when what we do for God, however small it seems, contributes to the fulfilment of his purposes in the future.

And that also means that he has specific things for us to do: perhaps a career to follow, a person to help, or a spiritual gift to use.

To think about *How can we set about discovering and doing God's purposes?*

Postscript *Knowing God personally involves learning about him from the Bible as well as experiencing him in our lives.*

6:1–5
A loving God: John 3:16; 2 Thessalonians 2:16,17; 1 John 4:10–12
A purposeful God: Ephesians 1:9–12; 3:3

BIBLE SUMMARY

Walking with God

'Enoch walked with God' (Genesis 5:22). 'Walking with God' means keeping him always in mind, aware of his purposes and reflecting his character. It implies patience too, in not running ahead to do something which might seem right, but is wrong in God's timing.

Walking in faith

Abraham is a good example of a faithful relationship to God. He believed God when he was told his wife would have a son, even though it was many years before the boy was born (Hebrews 11:8–12).

Then, later on, he obeyed God even at such extreme times of testing as when God told him to prepare to sacrifice his son Isaac. God saved the boy at the last minute, and praised Abraham for his faith (Hebrews 11:17–19; Genesis 22:1–19).

Walking in light

John, one of Jesus' closest followers, said we should 'walk in the light, as he (Jesus) is in the light' (1 John 1:7). 'Light' means 'God's truth and holiness'.

As we allow his 'light' to expose our sinfulness and make clear how we should live, we begin to enjoy deep Christian friendship (or 'fellowship') with others and experience the forgiveness and help of God.

Walking by the Spirit

Paul said that a Christian could either 'gratify the desires of the sinful nature' or walk 'by the Spirit' (Galatians 5:16). Our natural tendency towards self-centred living is not God's way, he said. So in order to overcome it, he told his readers to live in daily dependence on the Holy Spirit who dwells in their lives (Galatians 5:25).

To think and pray about *Walking with God requires patience, trust, honesty and perseverance. How can we grow in our experience of these things?*

FOOTSTEPS IN THE SNOW (Robert F. Hicks)
Walking with God means being a follower – a disciple of Jesus. A disciple not only follows his master's teaching but also endeavours to live like him.

KNOW YOUR ENEMY

The key truth *The Christian is confronted by forces which threaten to hinder or destroy his relationship with God.*

The world

The physical universe was created by God, and although it shares in the effects of man's sinfulness, it is not itself an evil place as some people have thought.

However, the world which people have created, the world of social, business and political life, is often organised without any concern for God and his laws.

The Bible warns us that this 'world' has attitudes and beliefs contrary to Christianity. It is frequently more concerned with getting than giving. It may regard as right what God says is wrong. Jesus said that although we do not belong to this world but to his kingdom, we are nevertheless called to serve him in it.

To think about *What aspects of human society do you think pose the greatest challenge to Christians?*

The flesh

Whenever the New Testament refers to 'flesh' as something sinful, it does not mean the physical body, but our natural selfishness. It is often translated 'sinful nature'. This is the 'old nature' which Jesus seeks to replace with his love.

Sometimes, when there is an opportunity to do something positive for God, we will feel lazy or tired, or try to get it done easily by not doing it properly. That feeling is the 'flesh' resisting the Holy Spirit within us.

And sometimes we will feel a strong urge just to indulge ourselves no matter what the cost to us or to others. That, too, is a fleshly desire which God wants us to resist.

BIBLE CHECK

The world: John 17:15–18; 1 John 2:15–17
The flesh: Matthew 26:41; Galatians 5:15–25

To think about *What particular sins of the flesh are you most likely to face in your locality, and how could you conquer the temptations?*

The adversary

The Bible is in no doubt about the existence of a personal evil spirit called the devil (see next page). Some forms of opposition to the Christian life are especially associated with him.

First, there is temptation to do wrong, or perhaps to use wrong means to achieve God's purposes. Then there are doubt and lack of faith which hinder our effectiveness for God. And finally there is personal conflict in the church which ruins our witness of love.

Sometimes, other people do the devil's work for him; by ridiculing our faith, opposing the work of the church, and even persecuting Christians.

To think about *How do you think God expects us to fight our spiritual warfare against evil forces?*

The last enemy

Death is described in scripture as 'the last enemy'. It is a barrier through which we have to pass before we can enter eternal life in God's presence.

Jesus has already passed through death and come back to life again – he has defeated this enemy so that it cannot prevent us entering heaven.

But we must still die. The Christian has nothing to fear from death itself, although the act of dying is often a sad and sometimes a frightening occasion. It reminds us of the weakness of human life which will only be restored in heaven.

To think about *What comfort, encouragement and hope are available for the Christian facing death?*

Postscript *Although Christians face opposition from many directions, they need never be defeated because the power of God is greater than all their enemies.*

The adversary: Mark 8:31–33; 1 Peter 5:8,9; Ephesians 6:11,12
The last enemy: 1 Corinthians 15:53–58; Philippians 1:21–24

BIBLE SUMMARY

The devil still roars
The devil, sometimes called Satan or the adversary, appears right at the start of the Bible narrative, when he tricks Adam and Eve into disobeying God (Genesis 3:1–7). He is always around, prompting people into wrong courses of action (e.g. 1 Chronicles 21:1,7), until he will be finally destroyed at the end of time by God (Revelation 20:10).

The spiritual being
The Bible does not speculate about the origin of Satan. The main clues are in Isaiah 14:12–17, Luke 10:18 and 2 Peter 2:4, which imply that he is a spiritual being (or angel) who rebelled against God. Sometimes he is shown as being in God's presence, opposing his plans (Job 1:6,7; Zechariah 3:1,2).

An evil being
His sole purpose is to destroy or hinder God's work (1 Peter 5:8,9). So he tried to make Jesus stray from God's path (Matthew 4:1–10).

Sometimes he tempts people in subtle ways, disguising his real motives and character by plausible ideas (2 Corinthians 11:14). At other times his opposition is clear and his attack direct, as when he takes total control of people as in Mark 5:1–13.

A dying being
He cannot possess those who are already indwelt by God's Spirit, although he can tempt them and if they are not careful, defeat them. But Jesus' death on the cross has already sealed his fate. His power is limited – like that of a wild animal tied to a rope – and he will never get what he wants. He is no match for God.

To think and pray about *If Jesus has already broken Satan's hold over people, what does that tell us about Satan's influence over our lives?*

CROSS ON A HILL OUTSIDE LAS VEGAS
(Robert F. Hicks)
Jesus' death on the cross is the guarantee of victory for Christians as well as demonstrating the defeat of sin, death and Satan.

KNOWING WHERE YOU STAND

The key truth *God wants us to be sure about the permanence of his love.*

Saved for ever

A person who saves someone from drowning does not let go of them if they struggle in fear. Neither will God let go of us, even if at times we struggle to get away from him.

Because we have been 'born again' or adopted into God's family, we have become new people. We will never be the same again. We were 'saved' when we received Jesus, and all who receive him have been given the unbreakable promise of eternal life.

We cannot lose that life; it cannot be taken from us. It depends, not on us living perfectly, but on God who cannot lie.

To think about *What effects can this assurance have on a Christian's daily life?*

Kept from falling

God's promise does not refer only to life after death. He does not keep us safe just for heaven. He wants to keep us close to him all through our lives, too.

He promises to protect us in situations which we could otherwise not cope with, although he will often allow us to be stretched beyond what we believe our limits to be. And when we are tempted, he offers the strength to say 'no'.

The Bible often refers to God as a fortress. The person who trusts him is safe and will not be defeated, however hard the battle around him.

To think about *What should Christians do when they find themselves in difficult situations?*

BIBLE CHECK
Saved for ever: John 6:38–40; Romans 8:1,2,38,39
Kept from falling: Matthew 6:13; Jude 24; Psalm 59:9,16,17

Equipped for victory

All we have thought about may make the Christian life sound negative and passive. Certainly, we do need to be realistic about the strength of the opposition we face and the impossibility of our withstanding it unless we depend entirely on God.

However, being a Christian is in fact a very positive way of living. It is actually an assault on the enemies of God. Having got our defences in order, we can go on the attack.

Jesus promises victory – over temptation, difficulty, and all opposition. We can work for these victories through prayer, by applying the truth of the Bible, telling others about Jesus, and by careful avoidance of sin.

To think about *Recall a well-known story (real or fictitious) which you have found inspiring about conquest over evil. What parallels does it have with the Christian life?*

Constantly forgiven

In Jesus' country, which was hot and dusty, people used to wash the feet of their visitors when they arrived. Once, when Jesus did this to his closest followers, he said, 'A person who has had a bath needs only to wash his feet; his whole body is clean'.

Christians have 'had a bath' in the forgiving love of God before setting out on the Christian life. But like the travellers, they can pick up 'dust and dirt' – sin – along the way, which needs to be forgiven and regularly washed out of their lives.

God promises to keep on forgiving and renewing us throughout our lives. But he also expects us to avoid sin as if it were a horrifying disease.

To think about *What should a Christian do as soon as he or she becomes aware of having sinned against God?*

Postscript *Because we can be confident about our relationship with God, we can serve him boldly and confidently, too.*

Equipped for victory: Psalm 98:1,2; 1 Timothy 6:11,12; 1 John 5:4,5
Constantly forgiven: John 13:8–11; 1 John 2:1,2; Matthew 6:14,15

BIBLE SUMMARY

The unforgivable sin

Occasionally some Christians become convinced that they have commited such a bad sin that they can never be forgiven. However, their very concern shows they *can* still be forgiven, because they know they have done wrong and are concerned about it. The only person whom God cannot forgive is the one who will not admit his need of that forgiveness (1 John 1:6).

Blasphemy against the Spirit

Jesus did say that there was one unforgivable sin (Matthew 12:31). He called it 'blasphemy against the Spirit'.

Blasphemy against the Holy Spirit is deliberately (not just mistakenly) attributing to Satan the work of God. Only a person totally opposed to God can say that. He will never want forgiveness, and so will not get it.

Apostasy

Hebrews 6:4–8 says that a person who has experienced Jesus' new life cannot be forgiven if he commits 'apostasy'. This is much more than, say, Peter's denial of Jesus (Mark 14:66–72). Peter was forgiven.

Apostasy describes the action of a person who leaves the family of God (of which they were not true members) and then seeks to destroy it. Such a person is unable to receive anything God offers.

Not guilty

Sometimes, Christians become depressed because their feelings of guilt are so strong and they feel they cannot be forgiven. Jesus not only forgives, but washes away our guilt. We need to forgive ourselves, and not sink under a weight of guilt. (See Psalm 103:1–14.)

To think and pray about *'There but for the grace of God go I': think of times when the gracious care of God has kept you or someone you know faithful to him, and thank him.*

SHEEP, NORTH WALES (Robert G. Hunt)
Jesus said, 'My sheep listen to my voice . . . and they follow me. I give them eternal life.' Christian assurance will never be lacking as long as we are 'listening' and 'following'.

KNOWING THE TRUTH

The key truth *The Christian life is based on the truth God has shown to us, and he wants us to put that truth into practice.*

Set free by truth

Jesus once said, 'You will know the truth, and the truth will set you free' (John 8:32). When we have accepted God's truth about ourselves, our needs, and Jesus' death, we are set free from the prison of sin: it cannot separate us any longer from God's love.

We are also set free from ourselves. Jesus offers us the help we need to overcome the faults and failings which hurt others but which we have been powerless to change.

And he sets us free from Satan's clutches, too. The powers of evil may attack us, but they can no longer harm us.

To think about *What steps do you need to take in order to experience the freedom of Jesus?*

Surrounded by truth

Everyone knows that there are right and wrong ways of doing certain things, like building a house. If the rules are not followed, the house will fall down.

God created people to live according to certain rules. They are summarised in the ten commandments. They are like a moral and spiritual guidebook. They tell us to love God, care for others, and look after the things he has given us.

Far from being restrictive, preventing us from doing what we would like, God's truthful laws are like the fence at the top of a steep cliff. They prevent us from harming ourselves and each other.

BIBLE CHECK
Set free by truth: John 8:31–36; John 14:6; Galatians 5:1
Surrounded by truth: Exodus 20:1–17; Matthew 5:17–20

To think about *How would you answer the person who says that God's laws are out of date and unnecessary?*

Taught by the truth

The best way to find out the truth about someone is to question them personally and compare their answers with what others say about them.

God promised that because Christians know him personally, they will also understand and know the truth about him, his world and purposes. But we do not suddenly receive a whole library of knowledge when we become Christians.

As God teaches us in our experience, we have to check that experience against what the Bible says. God's Word always reflects God's truth, whereas our experience – or our understanding of it – may be imperfect.

To think about *How can knowledge of the truth be turned into practice of the truth?*

Inspired by truth

Jesus often found himself in difficult situations. So, too, did his first followers. But they never tried to get out of them by telling lies.

When Peter told a lie about his relationship with Jesus (he denied he knew him, just when Jesus needed his support), he deeply regretted it. King David in the Old Testament used trickery and murder to get what he wanted, and he was punished by God.

The whole Christian life is based on truth. God never does wrong, nor does he lead his people to do wrong. He expects us to think, speak and act honestly, even if others around us do not.

To think about *What might be the consequences of being truthful in a situation where others want to lie and deceive?*

Postscript *It is easier to be truthful in practice if we are also thinking truthfully in our minds.*

Taught by the truth: Psalm 119:9–16; John 17:17; 1 John 2:20–22
Inspired by truth: Ephesians 4:25; 1 Peter 2:22

BIBLE SUMMARY

Law and grace

Paul's letter to the Galatians, like most of the New Testament letters, was written to meet a special need. The Christians in Galatia had started to make fresh rules for new converts to follow (Galatians 1:6–9). So Paul explains the uses and limits of rules in the Christian life.

Faith is the key

The Christian life begins by trusting (or having faith in) Jesus Christ and in all he has done. We cannot have a right relationship with God just by keeping his rules, because in fact we have broken at least some of them already (2:16; 3:6).

Jesus has saved us from the law which demanded that we pay in full the punishment for our sins (3:10–14).

The law came first

God's law was given centuries before Christ came to earth. It was meant to help people understand God's nature and how they should live (3:19, 23–26). It was a temporary measure until Jesus came to deal with it and give God's final teaching to mankind (4:4–7).

Rules out; obedience in

The Christian life is not the product of detailed man-made rules about behaviour, or of superstitious ritual (4:8–10). However, that does not mean that the Christian can do anything he likes; the Holy Spirit helps us to live in obedience to God's will (5:1, 13–24).

To think and pray about *How can we achieve a balance between unnecessary regulations and unchecked freedom?*

STUDYING JOYFULLY (Adrian Neilson)
The relationship between truth and freedom should encourage us joyfully to read and study God's Word, knowing that it can only enrich our lives and equip us for living.

KNOWING YOUR PRIVILEGES

The key truth *God has given us many privileges to inspire and encourage us in our Christian lives.*

Belonging to God's family

The 'family' of God – all those who love and serve him – is not restricted to one place. It extends across the whole world. And it stretches right back into history.

Belonging to such a well-established group is a privilege because we know that as members of it we are right at the centre of God's purposes for the world.

And it is an encouragement because we can look back on how other Christians have triumphed over temptation and conquered evil. From their example we can learn how to live Christian lives, and know that what we face has been faced before – and God's power seen in it.

To think about *'There is nothing new under the sun!' Think of ways in which other people's experiences can help and teach you.*

Being an ambassador

An ambassador is a person chosen to represent his country's interest in a foreign land. He tells people what his country believes, and he helps his fellow-countrymen when they visit that land.

Every Christian is an ambassador for Christ, representing his kingdom in a 'foreign' land – a society which does not care much for him.

That means our first loyalty is to Jesus. Christians will always try to live as he wants, rather than follow the standards of the world around them. And their duties never stop; they are ambassadors wherever they go. People will judge our Lord by what we do and say.

To think about *List the duties of an ambassador and discuss how they apply to a Christian life.*

BIBLE CHECK
Belonging to God's family: Romans 8:15,16; Hebrews 11:32–12:2

Bearing good news

The Christian is a messenger as well as an ambassador. We have been given a message to pass on to other people; the message, or good news, of Jesus' life, death and resurrection.

The Christian faith is not something to be kept secret. Jesus told us to proclaim it to all who will listen. God is concerned for everyone, everywhere.

Not all Christians have a special gift for preaching or teaching. But everyone can tell others the simple facts that God cares for them and can be known by them. It is a message the world badly needs to hear, because so many people feel lost or anxious, and do not have the joy of knowing God.

To think about *What are the things God has done for you? How would you tell others about them?*

Becoming a saint

People often think of saints as very holy men and women who did miracles and who have statues or pictures made of them.

But the Bible calls every Christian believer a saint. One of our privileges is being regarded so highly by God. The trouble is, we are not always very saintly people!

So we are called to *live* as saints – to grow in our faith and understanding so that we shall actually be what God has intended we should be. It is not a matter of whether or not we feel saintly, nor of adopting an artificial air of other-worldliness. Rather, we are simply to reflect the love of Jesus through our daily lives.

To think about *Holiness means 'set apart for God'; what are its chief characteristics?*

Postscript *It is easy to take our privileges for granted, so it helps if we thank God for them regularly.*

Being an ambassador: 2 Corinthians 5:20; Ephesians 6:18–20
Bearing good news: Acts 8:4; 2 Kings 7:3–10; Luke 8:38,39
Becoming a saint: Colossians 1:1–4; Philippians 2:1–13

BIBLE SUMMARY

Who is on the Lord's side?

Joshua had what seemed to be an impossible task ahead.
Moses, the man who led Israel out of slavery in Egypt,
was dead. And Joshua had the job of helping a vast
number of people settle into a new country (Joshua
1:1–5).

But he was promised the power of God, who had
not failed Moses (1:5). His own courage was to be
strengthened by reading the scriptures (1:8,9).

Promises, promises

As God's people moved into the new land, they were
told to keep God's commands and do things his way.
At first they promised to do so (1:16–18), but they soon
forgot what they had said (7:10–15).

But not Joshua. At the end of his life, having gone
through many difficulties and suffered many disap-
pointments, his faith remained as strong as ever.
'Choose for yourselves this day whom you will serve,'
he said – either the false gods or the real God. 'But as
for me and my household,' he added, 'we will serve the
Lord' (24:15). The privilege of serving God dominated
his whole life.

To think and pray about

Who is on the Lord's side?
Who will serve the King?
Who will be his helpers
Other lives to bring?
Who will leave the world's side?
Who will face the foe?
Who is on the Lord's side?
Who for him will go?

Growing

The life that God wants us to live is not an exchange – his life for ours – but a union of his life in and with ours.

To a large extent we grow into what we want to become. The more we want to become like Jesus, learning from him, the more we will grow; and we have the promise of God's help. In growing we shall see . . .

The necessity for growth
The root and fruit of growth
Practical demonstrations of growth
The secret and pattern for growth
The problems to be faced when growing.

MATTERHORN REFLECTED (Adrian Neilson)

THE NEED FOR GROWTH

The key truth *However long a person has been a Christian, they still have more to learn and experience of God's love and purposes.*

Growing into Christ

If anyone wants to know exactly what living a Christian life involves, they need only read the accounts of Jesus' life. Neither his enemies nor his closest friends could point to any wrong actions or words.

He is the example we are to follow, the standard by which our words and deeds can be measured. When faced with a difficult decision, it is often helpful to ask, 'What would Jesus have done if he was here?'

But we are not only to grow more like him. The Bible reminds us of the need to grow closer to him personally: to love him more dearly and serve him more faithfully.

To think about *What practical steps will help you become more like Jesus?*

Growing in faith

As a friendship with someone develops, so too does the trust between the two people. The Christian learns steadily how to trust Jesus, and so his or her faith grows stronger.

God has given us many promises: to help, provide, lead, teach and protect his followers. Most Christians find it helpful to take God at his word in one or two small things. Then, as they learn to trust him and apply his truth, they can move on to bigger things.

But God is not like an automatic machine giving us whatever we ask. His promises relate to his purposes for us, so growing in faith also involves discovering his will.

To think about *'What he has done for others, he will do*

BIBLE CHECK
Growing into Christ: Ephesians 4:15; 1 Peter 2:21–23
Growing in faith: Luke 17:5; 2 Corinthians 10:15; 2 Thes-

for you.' What facts can you think of which show whether or not this is always true?

Growing in knowledge

'Knowledge' in the Bible often means 'understanding' or even 'experience', rather than simply 'knowing facts'. Knowing God involves growing not only in Bible knowledge, but also in understanding his will.

In a human friendship a person may know instinctively how the other feels or what they want. The aim of the Christian life is to develop a deep awareness of God's general purposes, so that we can discover more easily what he specifically wants in each situation.

This understanding grows through prayer, Bible reading, worship, and the willingness to put Jesus first in everything.

To think about *Humility is aware of its ignorance; pride assumes it knows all things. How can we develop a truly humble approach to God and his will?*

Growing in love

One of the hardest parts of the Christian life is allowing Jesus to change our habits and attitudes, and especially our relationships with other people. The selfishness which prefers to dominate others, rather than submit to them, dies hard.

So every Christian has to grow in love, by learning how to say sorry, how to care for others, and how to be kind even to those who hate or despise in return.

The rule for Christian living is God first, others second, and self last. And to apply that, we need the help of the Holy Spirit. The standard is too high to achieve on our own.

To think about *What examples has Jesus given us of unselfish love towards other people?*

Postscript *A growing person does not have to wait until he reaches a certain stage before he can be useful to God; serving him is in fact an important aid to growth.*

---

salonians 1:3
Growing in knowledge: Colossians 1:9,10; 2 Peter 3:18
Growing in love: 1 Thessalonians 3:12,13; 4:9–12

BIBLE SUMMARY

Becoming like Jesus

Christians are sometimes – and usually wrongly – accused of being a closed group of people who conform to certain customs. Like the rest of God's creation, there is enormous variety among Christians. As we grow in our faith, we begin to conform not to each other but to the character of Jesus.

Our nature renewed

The Bible teaches that every human being is created in the image of God (Genesis 1:26). But human sinfulness has damaged and distorted our likeness to God.

During the Christian life the damage is slowly repaired by the Holy Spirit (Colossians 3:9,10), and our whole self is finally and completely renewed in heaven (1 John 3:2).

God's will for us

Every Christian aims to be like Jesus – and every non-Christian expects us to be like him! The process of becoming like him – honouring God in all that we do – is sometimes called 'sanctification', or growth in holiness (1 Thessalonians 4:3). The Holy Spirit will point out things in our lives which need correcting (John 16:8). And, like growing children, there are certain things we can do to aid this process.

The Bible is called 'food' or 'milk', and so we can draw spiritual nourishment from it (1 Peter 2:2). Using the gifts which God has given us is like exercising our bodies (1 Corinthians 9:26,27; Ephesians 4:11–16). And keeping in touch with God through prayer is like breathing fresh air (Ephesians 6:18).

To think and pray about *Our personal growth also affects other Christians. How can we help or hinder their faith by the way we live?*

SUNSET REFLECTED IN A LAKE (Robert F Hicks)
The Bible promises that we can experience a constant transformation as we open our whole being to Jesus Christ, becoming more like him.

THE SOURCE OF GROWTH

The key truth *The Holy Spirit is the source and inspiration of all Christian growth.*

The Spirit lives in us

The Christian is like a house with many 'rooms' – he or she is a person with many interests, relationships and talents. When we become Christians, the Holy Spirit enters our house – our lives.

Slowly he moves from part to part clearing away the dust of sin, opening up the windows of the mind so that God's light can shine in, and fills us with new life.

But he does not always break down locked doors. He dwells within us, but may not have access to every part, unless we invite him in to do his work, and help us grow as Christians.

To think about *How would you try to help someone who found it hard to hand some part of their life over to the Holy Spirit?*

The Spirit sanctifies us

The Holy Spirit wants to make us 'holy' – people reflecting the love and goodness of God. He does this in three ways.

First, he points out what is wrong in our life, perhaps through our conscience, some Bible passage, or even through another person. Then he gives his help and strength to overcome that sin or habit.

And thirdly, he replaces sinful words and actions with what the Bible calls the 'fruit of the Spirit'. These are positive attitudes such as love and patience which are expressed in practical service to God and other people.

BIBLE CHECK
The Spirit lives in us: Revelation 3:20; John 14:16,17
The Spirit sanctifies us: Ephesians 4:30; 1 Peter 1:14–16

To think about *The Bible speaks of the 'splendour of holiness'; what does this phrase mean and describe?*

The Spirit empowers us

The New Testament word for the power the Holy Spirit gives us is *dunamis*, from which comes the word for dynamite. His power can be explosive!

Sometimes he will blast away things that stand in the way of God. He will break down barriers which other people set up in order to protect themselves from the gospel of Jesus Christ.

But often, his power is also experienced when he gives us patience to endure suffering, or strength of character and wisdom to do a difficult task. He can be powerful as dynamite; he can also be gentle as a dove.

To think about *For what do we especially need God's power today?*

The Spirit unites us

Each Christian is a member of God's family, but like ordinary human families, the members do not always get on well with each other. In fact, the family is broken up by many differences of opinion.

But the Holy Spirit is concerned to help us show our faith by working together despite our differences. That is why he gives special abilities or 'gifts' to Christians, so that we can both give to and receive from each other some spiritual truth.

The Spirit also 'reconciles' people: he helps to heal broken relationships, and brings love and peace to situations where before there was hate and discord.

To think about *What actions on our part would contribute most to the Spirit's work of uniting God's people?*

Postscript *Growing in the Christian life involves submission to the Holy Spirit, and also willingness to learn from other Christians.*

The Spirit empowers us: Romans 15:13,17–19; Ephesians 3:20; 2 Timothy 1:7
The Spirit unites us: Ephesians 4:3; 1 Corinthians 1:10–13

BIBLE SUMMARY

The fruit of the Spirit

One of the simplest, most beautiful but also most demanding of descriptions of the Christian is found in Paul's letter to the Galatians (5:22,23). He lists nine virtues, which he calls 'the fruit of the Spirit', which cannot be produced merely by our own effort, but are the result of God's work in our lives (compare John 15:1–8). This is what they mean:

Love towards God

'Love' means self-sacrificing devotion to God. 'Joy' refers to our thankfulness for all that he has done for us through Jesus, and 'peace' reminds us of our healed relationship with him. As these fruits grow in us, we are likely to become more loving, joyful and peaceable people, bringing a sense of God's presence to others.

Patience towards people

'Patience' is the virtue of keeping calm with people who are aggressive or thoughtless in their attitude towards us. 'Kindness' means being thoughtful and sensitive about people's needs. And 'goodness' is the willingness to help people practically with no thought about the cost to ourselves.

At peace with ourselves

The Christian becomes 'faithful' in the sense of being someone others can trust not to let them down. He is 'gentle', too, which implies being humble, reasonable, considerate, and unselfish. And finally, the Christian is 'self-controlled', experiencing the power of God's Spirit in every area of human weakness.

To think and pray about *What would your church or town be like if everyone was demonstrating the fruit of the Spirit? How might you encourage them to?*

YOUTH CLIMBING (Robert F Hicks)
Life with God is an adventure that takes on a threefold dimension – love towards God; patience towards others; peace within ourselves. This is an evidence of the work of the Spirit in our union with Christ.

THE EVIDENCE OF GROWTH

The key truth *Christian growth can be noticed by the steady changes which take place in a person's life.*

A growing experience

Jesus is alive! That has been the cry of Christians in every generation. They believe it for two reasons. One is that they can point to the historical certainty that Jesus rose from the dead.

And the other is that they can see evidence of his influence in their lives. Looking back, they can see how he has helped them overcome sin and temptation.

But above all, they can recall times when God has acted in some way in their lives: answering prayers, using their words or actions to encourage other Christians or to bring people to Christ, and showing he is in control in some difficulty or problem.

To think about *We can experience God's help in small as well as large things; think of your own experiences, and share them with someone else who will understand and rejoice with you.*

A growing confidence

As we begin to see God at work in our own lives and in the lives of others around us, our confidence in God's promises and power will increase, and our fears will decrease. As that happens, we will be encouraged to ask him to do greater things.

The New Testament often speaks of boldness in approaching God and in attempting things for him.

But of course, Christian confidence is always in what God is both able and willing to do. There is no place in the Christian life for the kind of over-confidence which is not humbly depending on God at all times.

To think about *The disciples 'spoke the word of God boldly' only weeks after running away in fear at Jesus' crucifixion. What made them change?*

BIBLE CHECK
A growing experience: 1 Corinthians 15:3–8; Acts 12:5–11
A growing confidence: Ephesians 3:12; 6:19,20

A growing usefulness

God has something for each Christian to do. It may be a specific job within the church – preaching, or counselling others. It may be showing his love in appropriate ways in our ordinary daily life.

The Holy Spirit has showered all kinds of 'gifts' on the church, which those who receive them are to use for the benefit of everyone else. Teachers and preachers, artists and administrators, people who can organise and others who can help.

One of the Bible's most touching stories of usefulness is that of John Mark. He found the going too hard while travelling with Paul, who later refused to take him back, even though others trusted him. But at the end of his life Paul called for Mark, saying how useful he was.

To think about *How would you set about discovering the gifts God has given you?*

A growing battle

Shortly after Jesus was baptised by John the Baptist at the start of his public ministry, he experienced severe temptation. It is a common experience. Great blessing is sometimes followed by tough spiritual warfare and testing.

It has been said that the devil only concerns himself with those who threaten his temporary hold on the world. A Christian determined to serve Jesus is just such a threat.

And so the growing Christian may also find himself a fighting Christian; the battle gets hotter as faith grows stronger.

To think about *If the strongest always wins, what hope does the Christian have as he faces spiritual warfare?*

Postscript *The Christian will be encouraged by becoming aware of growth, but the person who spends time looking for growth is likely to become self-centred.*

A growing usefulness: Acts 13:13; 15:37–40; 2 Timothy 4:11; Romans 12:4–8

A growing battle: 2 Corinthians 2:10,11; 1 Thessalonians 2:17,18

BIBLE SUMMARY

The battle for the mind

A verse in the Old Testament book of Proverbs is translated in one Bible version like this: 'As he thinketh in his heart, so is he' (Proverbs 23:7, AV). Throughout the Bible the mind – our inner attitudes and real beliefs – is seen as the key to spiritual growth. If our thoughts are wrong, our actions can never be right (Matthew 7:17–20).

Become a non-conformist

Every group of people tends to have its own agreed standards and way of looking at things. In some cases these are quite opposite to Jesus' teaching. The world around may say, 'Take all you can get.' But Jesus said, 'Give all you have.'

So if we are going to lead a Christian life, we cannot always think in the same way as others (Romans 12:2). Jesus said that our old, sinful approach to life was to be finished with for ever (Mark 8:34–37).

Let your mind be renewed

The Bible never says 'don't' without also saying 'do'. So God remoulds our minds from the inside (Romans 12:2), putting in them his love and laws (Hebrews 10:15,16). At the same time, he tells us to concentrate on what is good, holy and of God (Philippians 4:8), and thus to develop renewed minds (Ephesians 4:22–24).

Our new way of thinking is characterised by the humility and concern which Jesus himself showed (Philippians 2:3–9). In fact, the Christian has the privilege of being given insight into Jesus' own mind (1 Corinthians 2:15,16).

To think and pray about *What are the main attitudes towards God and his truth in your society, and how do they differ from a Christian view?*

AFRICAN CHRISTIAN STUDENTS (Peter Heaps)
As Christians it is important not only to increase our understanding of the faith, but also to ensure the daily renewing of our minds.

THE SECRET OF GROWTH

The key truth *Prayer is the chief means by which Christians maintain and develop their relationship with God.*

In touch with God's purposes

A person taking part in a major activity involving many others needs to keep in touch with the organiser. He needs to know exactly what job he wants him to do.

Prayer is a way of keeping in touch with what God wants us to do. If we pray in accordance with his purposes, then he promises to give what we ask at the right time. But if we neglect prayer, it is easy to stray from his plan.

Prayer is nothing more nor less than conversation with God. It is a natural and important part of our relationship with him. What is more, he really wants to hear from us!

To think about *Discuss how much conversation affects human friendships. What does this tell you about the value of prayer?*

Aware of God's presence

If you are talking to a person, it is impossible not to be aware of his presence! But when we pray, it is sometimes helpful to repeat Jesus' promise, 'I am with you always'; he *is* present, although we cannot see him.

Sometimes, when we pray, we will feel him near us, perhaps almost with a physical sensation, or by a deep awareness inside.

But what we feel is less important than what prayer actually does. It brings us close to God. Jesus, through his death, has broken down the invisible barrier of sin which once had barred us from God's presence. Now, the simplest prayer is like having a personal audience with a king, who cares for us and longs to help us.

To think about *Recall some of the words which best de-*

BIBLE CHECK
In touch with God's purposes: 1 John 5:14,15; 1 Timothy 2:1–6

scribe God. How will those aspects of his nature affect the prayers we bring to him?

A source of God's power

Some remarkable things happened when Jesus' early followers prayed. Many people became Christians through their preaching. Others were healed of their diseases. Peter and Paul were both released from prison by God's powerful intervention as a result of prayer.

Even Jesus prayed, sometimes all night, and he told his followers that some works of God could only be achieved by concentrated periods of prayer which were not stopped even for food.

It is often true that the prayerless Christian is a powerless Christian. God sometimes chooses to channel his power to us and others when we pray.

To think about *What sort of power does God give to those who pray?*

Taking time to pray

Jesus sometimes looked for a quiet place away from all disturbances so that he could pray to his heavenly Father. His example is a good one to follow.

There is so much to talk to God about. And human nature (and the devil's temptings) can find all sorts of excuses for avoiding it. So it is often helpful to set aside a convenient time on most days to pray, just as you set aside time to eat. And keeping a list of things to pray about will help you to forget nothing.

Paul also reminded his readers to pray at all times. A brief prayer in the middle of the day, when we are especially conscious of our need for God's help, or when we are thinking of someone else, is important and effective.

To think about *What factors should you take into consideration in deciding when to have a regular time of prayer?*

Postscript *Every decision we take, every situation we are in, are legitimate subjects for prayer. But we are also told to pray for other people, that they too may know God's power.*

Aware of God's presence: Ephesians 3:11,12; Hebrews 10:19–22
A source of God's power: Mark 9:28,29; Acts 4:31–33
Taking time to pray: Psalm 5:1–3; Luke 6:12

BIBLE SUMMARY

What is prayer?

Prayer is often hard to understand, as well as to practise. But there are two important facts on which it depends.

Open to God

People sometimes ask why God wants us to pray for things when Jesus has said that he already knows our needs (Matthew 6:8). The main reason is that the act of asking implies a humble dependence on God, which is the basis of the Christian life (Matthew 6:8). God delights to give good gifts to those who ask him.

If we are able to receive his gifts humbly, we will be more likely to use them properly. Besides, while we pray we may realise we are asking for the wrong thing, so our prayers can be modified (James 4:3–10).

Deeply concerned

Prayer is, in a sense, very easy: just telling God, aloud or silently, how we feel or what we need. We don't even have to use special words. But in other ways it is hard; the prayer which God answers is often hard work, because it is part of our spiritual battle (Ephesians 6:18).

Also, in our praying it is important to mean what we say, sincerely asking for what we believe is his will for us – and to trust that God is actually able to do what we ask (Mark 11:22–25; James 1:6).

Some prayers consist of deep longing and groaning inside our hearts and minds, and cannot be fully expressed in words. But God still understands and answers them, because they are inspired by his Spirit (Romans 8:26,27).

To think and pray about *God sometimes uses us in answering our own prayers. Think of some situations in which this might happen.*

LEARNING TO SKI (Robert F. Hicks)
Prayer is proof that we are developing as Christians. The fact that sometimes we find it hard should not stop us from persevering.

A PATTERN FOR GROWTH

The key truth *Prayer consists of praising and thanking God, and being sorry for our wrongdoing, as well as asking for things.*

Love prayers

The friendship between God and the Christian is marked by love. Love grows between two people as they learn to express their feelings for each other. So the Christian grows as he or she experiences God's loving care and learns to express his love for him.

Our love prayers, or 'adoration' and worship, tell God we love him for all that he is and for all that he has done for us through Jesus Christ.

Such prayers help us to grow closer to him, deepen our appreciation of him, and keep us open to receiving his help and his gifts. The Psalms are full of love prayers, and many Christians find them helpful as a basis for their own.

To think about *Make a list of all the things for which Christians can love and praise God. Then praise him!*

Sorry prayers

The wrong things we do can grieve God, and make our relationship with him more difficult.

Each time we pray it is a good idea to start by telling God we are sorry for the sins we have committed. We can then experience his forgiveness in a fresh way, and can clear away the blockages which prevent us knowing his power.

We also need to be willing to say sorry to other people whom we have offended, and to forgive those who have wronged us. We can hardly be open to God's forgiveness if we are bitter and resentful towards other people.

BIBLE CHECK
Love prayers: Psalm 31:23; 95:1–7; 113:1–9

To think about *Why do we sometimes sin despite the help and power of God's Spirit?*

Thank you prayers

These are like love prayers, but they are a response to specific things that God has done for us or others.

We can thank him for answering our prayers, for providing for our needs, including things we take for granted yet still depend on him for, like a meal we are about to enjoy. We can also thank him for helping or guiding us, and for intervening in some situation.

Saying thank you before we ask for other things can help to increase our faith. It is a reminder of how much God has done already.

To think about *In what ways can we show our thankfulness to God, in addition to saying it?*

Asking prayers

These are the easiest and most common of all prayers but they should really come at the bottom of the list. It is a limited relationship which is expressed only in a series of requests or demands.

The Bible tells us to ask for three things. One is the spiritual resources and blessings God wants to share with us: deeper faith, knowledge of his will, the ability to obey him. Another is our daily needs – food, drink, clothes and shelter – because in many parts of the world people do not think of them as God's provision but as an automatic right.

And finally we are to ask for specific things: that someone we love will come to Jesus; that God will act in a situation, and for whatever he knows is good for us to have and enjoy.

To think about *How do you distinguish between the things you would like to have and the things which God wants you to have?*

Postscript *As we grow in the Christian life, prayer becomes more natural and spontaneous. It may sometimes grow stale unless we give each element its proper place.*

Sorry prayers: Matthew 6:14,15; Psalm 51
Thank you prayers: Psalm 116; Philippians 1:3–11
Asking prayers: Luke 11:9–13; James 1:5–7

BIBLE SUMMARY

Jesus' pattern for prayer

Jesus did not in fact teach a great deal about prayer; he told his followers to get on with it, because it is natural to talk to our heavenly Father. In 'The Lord's Prayer' (Matthew 6:7–15), however, he gave a **summary** of how and for what to pray, and not just a prayer to be recited.

Children and servants

First, we approach God as his children, remembering his greatness – 'Our Father in heaven . . .' and his holiness – 'hallowed be your name'. Then we ask that people all over the world will come to love, honour and serve him – 'your kingdom come', and that we ourselves may serve him faithfully – 'your will be done'.

Beggars and debtors

The next phrase reminds us to ask God to provide for our daily needs – nothing is too small for him – and to pray for the hungry and homeless – 'Give us today our daily bread.' Then we ask his forgiveness, and tell him we forgive those who have wronged us, just as Jesus forgave his murderers before his death – 'Forgive us our debts, as we also have forgiven our debtors.'

Guarded and kept

Finally, there is a reminder of our weakness: a prayer that God will protect us from the trials which will crush our faith – 'lead us not into temptation', and that he will release us from the power of Satan – 'deliver us from the evil one.'

To think and pray about *Consider each phrase of the Lord's Prayer, and explain it in your own words. Then turn those words into a simple prayer of your own.*

AFRICAN CHRISTIANS PRAYING (Peter Heaps)
As we pray we become involved with both God and man, by seeking God's kingdom in the lives of men.

THE PROBLEMS OF GROWTH

The key truth *The Christian life is not an escape route from difficulty, but a way through difficulty.*

Exercising faith

Jesus said that even a tiny amount of faith was all that was needed for God to work powerfully. But he also made it clear that he would not do great things if people did not believe he could.

Faith is not certainty, but trust. Growing as a Christian through prayer depends on our trusting God entirely to do what will most honour him, in his way and in his time.

Actually believing he will answer our prayers is not easy, but if we are too timid to ask, we may not see him work powerfully.

To think about *Why does God sometimes limit himself to working only in situations where his people really trust him?*

Waiting for answers

God is not always in a rush to do things, for he stands beyond time and is working out his purposes over many centuries. Sometimes we will have to wait a while before he answers our prayers.

This in itself can be a test of our faith: do we really want what we are asking for, and do we really believe Jesus can give it? He told us to keep on asking until we receive.

There are two things to do while we wait. One is to keep looking for an answer, which may be different to the one we expect. And the other is to make sure that all our prayers, and our whole life, are lined up with his will.

To think about *List those things which will help you to develop patience without losing interest or faith.*

BIBLE CHECK
Exercising faith: Luke 17:5,6; Matthew 13:57,58

Keeping alert

The person who wants to do things for Jesus Christ will always find opportunities – a word of explanation about their faith, an act of kindness, a job within the church. There will be challenges, too, and unexpected problems to face.

The Christian who is constantly in touch with God through prayer will be able to make the most of these opportunities and challenges. A short silent prayer at the time will keep our mind focused on him and help prevent us from relying on our own lesser abilities.

The example of Nehemiah in the Old Testament is a good one to follow. He and his helpers prayed quickly about their needs, then worked hard and sensibly at their jobs.

To think about *Discuss the various ways in which you can keep alert to see what God wants in each situation.*

When God seems silent

Many Christians experience times when God seems very far away, when their prayers seem to be unanswered, and when living the Christian life becomes hard and laborious.

It might be that they have sinned against God; maybe something in their life – a personal relationship, for example – needs sorting out. Or they may just be tired, or unwell.

But it might also be that God himself is leading them through what some have called 'the dark night of the soul'. It is a time when their longing for God deepens, and their faith is eventually strengthened, by being tested. Growing up in the Christian life, just like growing as a human person, is not all fun and games.

To think about *How would you reassure someone who feels that God has deserted them?*

Postscript *Jesus, says the Bible, was made perfect or complete through suffering. Those who obey him and follow him may find that he calls them to suffering, too, and through it to discover more of his love.*

Waiting for answers: Luke 18:1–8; James 5:7–11
Keeping alert: Nehemiah 2:4,5; 4:7–15; Proverbs 3:5–8
When God seems silent: Psalm 42:1–11; 38:9–22

BIBLE SUMMARY

God's mysterious ways

When something unexpected occurs, people often ask, 'Why has God allowed this to happen?' Usually it is a sort of complaint; they regard the event as undeserved punishment. But for the Christian, whatever happens can provide an opportunity to move forward in the Christian life, though the question 'Why?' may remain.

God's ways are different

Everyone knows that God is greater than any human being, so it is hardly surprising to read in the Bible that his ways and thoughts are beyond human understanding (Isaiah 55:8,9). They are too complex for us to work out (Ecclesiastes 3:11). That is why the Bible encourages us to pray carefully before making major decisions (see Jesus' example in Luke 6:12–16).

Human wisdom is limited

People usually do what they believe is right, but human wisdom can be very far from God's truth because it is not always informed by his law and will (1 Corinthians 2:3–10). Even Christians can be misled and mistaken (1 Corinthians 1:10–13; Galatians 1:6–9).

Despite this God promises to give us wisdom to know how to act correctly in each situation (James 1:5,6).

A new set of values

In fact, Jesus' teaching is often opposite to the accepted wisdom of the people around us. They usually say it is a sign of God's blessing to be rich; Jesus said it was a sign of his gracious love to be able to give to those in need at whatever cost to oneself (Matthew 5:42). We are so used to our Godless ways, that the Christian life can seem very strange and different.

To think and pray about *Faith involves trusting God without necessarily understanding him. But how can we be certain of his love when things seem to be going wrong?*

Discovering

Most great discoveries were made after many mistakes, and we should not be surprised or disappointed if we make mistakes. As we admit our failure we know that God forgives and understands. He wants us to live even more adventurously as we experience the richer, fuller life that comes to us as disciples of Jesus Christ.

In our progress as disciples we discover . . .

The dynamics of God's life
The clarity of God's way
The impact of God's will
The challenge of God's Word.

SIGNPOST ON THE WAY TO THE MATTERHORN
(Adrian Neilson)

DISCOVERING A NEW LIFE

The key truth *The Christian life is like a journey in which there are many things to be discovered.*

Journey into life

When Jesus first called a group of twelve men (known as the apostles) to follow him, they literally set off on a journey. Together they travelled around the land, teaching God's truth to all who would listen.

He used the picture of a journey to illustrate the Christian life. He said it is like turning off a broad, easy road of self-indulgence, because that way leads away from God.

Instead, the Christian way is a narrow, steep path. It has many obstacles and is sometimes hard going. But it leads to new life: a life lived in harmony with God, full of new joys and discoveries, which goes beyond death.

To think about *How would you explain to someone that the Christian life is not primarily about giving up things but discovering new ones?*

A constant companion

The Christian never walks alone. Even when we feel very lonely – perhaps when we are the only Christian in a place where others are hostile to our faith – God is always there.

He promises never to leave us. He will show us what he wants us to do, and how to do it.

He is like an expert guide. He knows the way through the difficulties which lie ahead. And he has many new things to show and teach us as we follow him into the sort of life he wants us to lead.

To think about *What is the basis for our confidence?*

BIBLE CHECK
Journey into life: Matthew 7:13,14; John 10:9,10
A constant companion: Psalm 23; Ephesians 3:14–21

New every morning

From time to time, ever since the days of the early church, people have claimed that God has given them a completely new teaching. They offer a new, improved version of Christianity. They either allow something which was previously forbidden in the Bible, or they insist on some custom being added to the gospel before a person can be fully recognised as a Christian.

But they are always wrong. God's purposes for his people, and his teaching, never change. Neither do his laws, nor the simple way of faith in Jesus through which we come to him.

His truths are always fresh, however. They never grow stale, and come to us 'new every morning'. Because Jesus is alive, he is always doing new things in us and for us.

To think about *What steps can you take to help keep your faith in Jesus always fresh?*

I know where I'm going

Some people who rightly recognise how great God is find it hard to understand that he is concerned with the details of their lives.

But he is – just how great he is! He not only forgives our sins and gives us eternal life, but he also has a special purpose for us in this life too.

That means the path we follow on our 'journey into life' has already been prepared by God. Life is not just a series of accidents; there is a plan to it. That plan is always good, although not always easy.

To think about *What is the difference between* **following** *God's will and* **resigning** *ourselves to it? Which are you doing?*

Postscript *Although there are many things to discover in the Christian life, the end is never in doubt: Jesus has prepared a place for us in heaven.*

New every morning: Ecclesiates 1:9; Lamentations 3:22,23; Galatians 1:6–9
I know where I'm going: Ephesians 2:10; Romans 12:2; Hebrews 13:20,21

BIBLE SUMMARY

Becoming a disciple

The word 'disciple' means a follower, one who learns from his teacher. Jesus does not want passive converts, but active disciples, people who will go on to discover the richness of the Christian life.

Jesus comes first

Jesus said that nothing should come between him and the Christian. Even family relationships would weaken our discipleship if they interfered with it (Luke 14:26). However, he made it clear that families were not to be neglected (Mark 7:9–13; John 19:26,27).

A rich person once asked what he had to do to become a follower of Jesus. Jesus told him to sell all his possessions and give the money to the poor. In his particular case, he would have done anything for Jesus except that. But Jesus made it clear that there can be no exceptions; love for Jesus is the Christian's priority. He wants us to put all that we have and are at his disposal (Luke 18:18–30, compare 9:23–25).

A willing sacrifice

Jesus does not require his followers to make sacrifices or give to the church in order to gain acceptance by God. Jesus' death was the ultimate sacrifice which brings God and people into harmony with each other (Hebrews 10:11–18).

But God does call us to offer ourselves as living sacrifices (Romans 12:1,2). That does not mean committing suicide, but being willing to do whatever Jesus wants, in the sure knowledge that his way is always best.

To think and pray about
'Send us out into the world in the power of your Spirit, to live and work to your praise and glory.' Think about what each phrase of this prayer means to you in your own words – then pray it!

AUTUMN PATH (Robert F. Hicks)
Autumn is a process of death giving place to winter, which is followed by spring. Similarly, as we follow Jesus, the process of dying to self produces the resurrected life of Christ as we live for others.

DISCOVERING GOD'S WAY

The key truth *God has shown us his unchanging purposes in several ways, so that we may be sure of what he wants.*

Shown through conscience

One aspect of being made 'in the image of God', as the Bible describes us, is that we know there are such things as right and wrong.

Unfortunately, the human conscience can be mistaken in what actually is right or wrong. It can be influenced by local customs and what we have been taught to believe.

But the Holy Spirit renews and revitalises the Christian's conscience. God's law slowly becomes more perfectly 'written on our hearts' so that we learn to tell instinctively what we should or should not do.

To think about *What can you do to attune your conscience to God's will?*

Shown through God's law

God has not laid down many rules and regulations for the Christian life. He wants us to love, serve and honour him freely, because we wish to and not because we feel we have to.

However, he has given a basic moral code, not just to Christians, but to all mankind. It is set out in the ten commandments (see next page).

These reflect the way God has made the world. They are the 'makers instructions' on how human life is designed to operate. We cannot expect to find peace and happiness if we break these laws, because we are destroying the very structure of peace and happiness itself.

BIBLE CHECK
Shown through conscience: Romans 2:14–16; Hebrews 9:13,14; 10:19–22

To think about *What would you say to someone who tells you he has broken one of God's laws?*

Shown through Jesus

Jesus Christ was God's final and most complete revelation of who he is and what he wants. In Jesus' life we find an example of how everyone should live, and in his teaching we discover God's principles for daily life.

Jesus showed that God's way has two vital elements. The first is loving and serving God at all times, and never compromising our faith.

The second is to love other people with the same kind of self-giving love which Jesus showed in his life, and especially on the cross. That means putting their interests before our own.

To think about *Discuss examples of how Jesus' teaching on loving our neighbour might be worked out in everyday life.*

Shown through the Bible

In the past, God revealed his will through people, often called prophets, and through Jesus' closest friends, the apostles. Their words are written in the Bible, through which God speaks today.

In the Bible we see how God's people in the past discovered his will, which never changes in principle, even if today's circumstances seem different.

The Bible is a permanent record of what God has said and done. Through it we can find out how he wants us to live, and what he wants us to avoid.

To think about *Why do you think the Bible is sometimes called 'the Word of God'?*

Postscript *God has promised to help us keep to his ways. If we trust our own abilities, we will fail, but if we draw on his power we can succeed.*

Shown through God's law: Exodus 20:1–17; Matthew 5:17–20
Shown through Jesus: John 13:15–17,34,35
Shown through the Bible: Romans 15:4; 2 Peter 3:1,2

BIBLE SUMMARY

The ten commandments
These ten brief instructions in Exodus 20:1–17 are the core of the Bible's teaching about our relationship to God and to one another. They fall into two sections.

Duty to God
The first four concern our approach to God. He is a God who saves his people (v.2; compare Jesus' work on the cross, Matthew 1:21). He cannot have any rival (v.3).

Because God is the mighty creator of the earth and is Lord over all creation (vs.5,6) people cannot, and should not, try to show what he looks like. Nor should we treat the power which belongs only to God as if it came from a lesser source (vs. 4,5). An 'idol' is anything we put in the place which God alone should have.

God is holy, and therefore is to be respected in word and deed (v.7). He has created people in such a way that they need to take one day in seven off work to relax and enjoy their God (vs.8–11).

Duty to others
Family life is something precious and to be preserved (v.12), because it is the basis of a stable society. That is why casual sexual realtions are forbidden (v.14); they weaken the family bond and deny the deep unity created between a married couple who share everything.

Human life is sacred and not to be taken (v.13), and the same applies to property belonging to others (v.15). We are not to lie for the sake of personal comfort or gain (v.16). And, as Jesus pointed out, the inner attitude is as important as the outward act (e.g. Matthew 5:21–30). So the wrong desires which could lead to theft, murder or adultery must be shunned.

To think and pray about *Discuss how these laws can be kept, and the ways people use to try to avoid them.*

MOTHER AND CHILD (Adrian Neilson)
God's law in the Ten Commandments was meant to bring us closer to himself and to one another. Family life at its best is a good example of this.

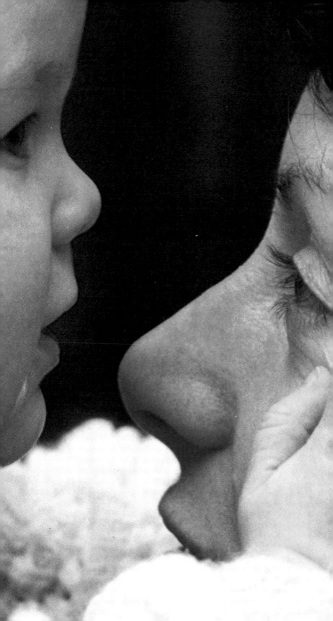

DISCOVERING GOD'S WILL

The key truth *God promises to guide us in every situation, so that we can do his will.*

Praying it through

When we want to find out God's specific purpose for us – whether it concerns the job we are to follow, a task to take on in church, or a problem we have to face – the first thing to do is pray specifically about it.

Jesus did this shortly before his crucifixion. Knowing he was about to be betrayed, and that death as a sacrifice for our sin would certainly follow, he prayed that God would spare him.

But he was determined to do only what God wanted, so he submitted to the Father's will. Through prayer, our will can be guided so that it matches God's will, and we can be strengthened to do it.

To think about *'Not my will, but yours be done.' How can we reach this point of submission to God?*

Searching the scriptures

The Bible is often the means God uses to guide us. Our reading of it will make us familiar with his general purposes.

But there will be times when a particular passage 'speaks' to us in a very clear way. It seems to fit exactly our situation. It may be a word of challenge to change something, or a word of encouragement to go ahead with a decision we are about to make.

It should not be used like a horoscope or magic oracle, however. People who dip into it at random can sometimes get a shock. One person who is supposed to have done that hit on the verses 'Judas went . . . and hanged himself' (Matthew 27:5) and 'Go and do likewise'! (Luke 10:37)

To think about *How can we make sure that we are using the Bible properly?*

BIBLE CHECK

Praying it through: Luke 22:39–46; Acts 10:9–16, 27–29

Talking it over
Big decisions are often made more easily after we have discussed them with an experienced Christian friend – perhaps a leader at our church.

Some people have a special insight into God's plans and our circumstances. Others are able to help us think through a situation, on the basis of their deeper experience of God. Sometimes their invitation to us to do something might in itself be sufficient guidance for us.

Even a casual remark, or perhaps a talk given at a church service or meeting, can be used by God to challenge and guide us.

To think about *How can you tell if another person's advice is likely to be trustworthy?*

Making up your mind
When the time comes to make a decision, some doubt may still remain in our minds. This might be for various reasons: our incomplete knowledge of the situation or even because God is testing our faith and our love for him.

There is no infallible rule. If the doubt persists, however, it is usually best not to act in the way proposed. Christians frequently – but not always – experience a sense of inner 'peace' when they reach a right decision. God's Spirit gives them the assurance that they are on the right track.

But such feelings should not be accepted on their own, because they can be wrong. And even with them, we still have to act 'in faith', trusting God to take us through to the next stage.

To think about *'It seemed good to the Holy Spirit and to us . . .' Summarise the steps which might lead to such a conclusion.*

Postscript *Sometimes our sin or self-will makes us unable to receive God's guidance. Then we need to ask him to make us willing to do whatever he says.*

Searching the Scriptures: Romans 15:4; 2 Peter 3:15,16
Talking it over: Acts 15:6–23; Galatians 2:11–16
Making up your mind: Acts 15:23–28; Romans 1:9–15

BIBLE SUMMARY

Living through faith

The Bible reminds us that Christians live by faith in Jesus rather than with certain, clear knowledge about the future (2 Corinthians 5:7). This means some decisions are made when we believe that they are what God desires, even if they seem unusual at the time (Hebrews 11:8). But faith is not folly; it is confidence that God has led us so far and will lead us on in the future (Hebrews 11:1,2). It does not mean we should stop using our minds!

God's common sense

One of the most obvious ways God guides us is through the circumstances we are in. The good Samaritan did not need to ask for guidance in Jesus' parable. He saw a man who had been beaten up and knew that, because of his need, God wanted him to stop and help. (Luke 10:33,34)

Similarly, Paul was often hindered from visiting Rome because of pressures to work in other places, although he longed to go there. In addition, the gospel had been preached in Rome already, so it would have been wrong to duplicate the effort. (Romans 15:22–29)

Using our gifts

Once, Jesus told a parable about the use of gifts or talents given to those who follow him (Matthew 25:14–30). It was clear that whether his servants had many or few, they all had the ability to use those gifts in the events of daily living.

He looks to us, also, to use the gifts and abilities we have. Even if they seem very small and insignificant to us, they are important to him (Matthew 10:40–42).

To think and pray about *Some decisions can be made quickly; others need time. How can you tell which is which?*

ENJOYING LIFE (Alan Hayward)
God's will for us is never meant to spoil the joy of living. Equally, we are meant to act responsibly as we discover the kind of lives he wants us to live.

DISCOVERING GOD'S WORD

The key truth *The Bible is the permanent record of God's revelation to mankind, and contains all we need to know for our new life in Jesus.*

A book of truth

The Bible is a unique book. Although it tells the stories of ordinary people and their experiences of God, it is much more than a religious biography.

It is uniquely 'inspired' by God. That means he guided the people who wrote it so that what they put down was a true record of God's nature and purposes.

Although the Bible contains 66 books written over some 1,500 years by more than 40 authors, it does not contradict itself. It contains different emphases, of course, and we see how God's revelation grew clearer through the years, but the truth it teaches is consistent.

To think about *What should be our reaction if we are told to do something by another Christian which is contrary to the teaching of the Bible? Discuss some such possible situations.*

A book of example

Although the Bible contains passages of pure teaching – some of Paul's letters, for example – most of it is about people.

Their surroundings were different from ours, but our feelings and problems are much the same as theirs were. So we can read stories of men and women who knew God well, and discover how they coped and remained faithful to him. They will challenge, excite and encourage us.

There are also examples of how not to live, and what mistakes to avoid. The people in the Bible were really human, ordinary people – warts and all!

To think about *Think of a well-known Bible story, e.g.*

BIBLE CHECK
A book of truth: John 17:17; 2 Timothy 3:14–17

Luke 10:25–37 or John 6. How can you apply its example or lesson in your own life?

A book of warning

The Bible includes books of 'prophecy'. They include Isaiah, Jeremiah, Ezekiel, Daniel and Amos in the Old Testament, and Revelation in the New Testament.

Occasionally, they foretell the future. Some of these prophecies have been fulfilled, some have yet to take place, and many apply to more than one period of history.

But the prophets were also God's messengers who warned his people that God was holy and just. They reminded them that they could not lead sinful lives and still receive God's help and favour, and they often spoke of God's judgement or punishment given even to those who claimed to serve him but who, in fact, were evil.

To think about *Why did God go to the trouble of warning his people of his anger? What do such passages teach us today?*

A book of challenge

The Bible presents us with two kinds of challenge. One is through great men and women of God, who challenge us by their total devotion to him.

The other is more direct. We are challenged by some of the writers to believe the truth which they have written down and to live lives which are worthy of God.

We are also challenged to take his message out into the world which prefers to ignore it. The Bible contains the truth which has brought us to faith in Jesus Christ, and it challenges us to take that message to others.

To think about *What help is available to enable us to rise to the challenges of the Bible?*

Postscript *The Bible is not a book to be read like any other. To hear God speaking to us through it, we will need to pray for the help of his Holy Spirit.*

A book of example: Hebrews 11:29–40; 12:1–4
A book of warning: Jeremiah 17:1–10; Revelation 2:1–7
A book of challenge: Mark 8:34–38; Luke 24:45–49

BIBLE SUMMARY

We need to know

The Bible contains all we need to know about God, Jesus, ourselves, and the world, in order to live Christian lives (2 Timothy 3:16,17). But it has often been ridiculed or questioned, even by Christian scholars.

Entirely trustworthy

The phrase 'inspired by God' in 2 Timothy 3:16 means 'breathed out by God' (see NIV: 'God-breathed'). God did not dictate his Bible to its authors, but guided their thoughts so that what they wrote was true and would encourage us to know, love and serve him.

The Bible contains all that we need to know in all matters of belief and behaviour (2 Timothy 3:15). If we follow what it says we can discover the reality of Jesus. It is also 'useful for teaching'; we do not need to add any man-made laws to it. The Holy Spirit who inspired it will interpret it to us (John 16:13–15; 2 Peter 1:20,21).

Not an encyclopaedia

The Bible does not contain all that there is to be known; about science, sport or sociology, for example. It does not even tell us everything about God; the universe would be too small to contain such knowledge!

Paul was dismayed that people were speculating about details which the Bible did not refer to (Colossians 2:8). The Bible speaks with authority about being a Christian and the content of Christian belief. Where it is silent, we are encouraged to trust God's wisdom in not revealing everything to us (1 Peter 1:10–12).

To think and pray about *The Bible can be understood by the least educated person, yet it will stretch the mind of the most intelligent. What does this tell you about what it says and how you can approach it?*

GAS LAMP IN SUNSET (Robert F. Hicks)
We need God's Word for our daily lives as well as the path before us. The Psalmist probably includes both in the famous verse 'Your word is a lamp to my feet (our daily lives) and a light for my path' (the future before us), Psalm 119:105.

APPLYING GOD'S WORD

The key truth *The Bible is a basic tool for the Christian life; by using it carefully we will keep close to God.*

Equipment for the journey

Just as no explorer would dream of leaving home without food, maps and a survival kit, so God does not expect us to go through life without some basic equipment which we will need on the way.

Our chief piece of equipment is the Bible. It provides wisdom for dealing with difficult situations, insight into the real needs of the world, and understanding of both God and his ways.

Above all, it provides us with spiritual 'food'. Our relationship with Jesus is nourished and enriched when we read and apply his Word. It draws us closer to our Guide.

To think about *Discuss the advantages of reading the Bible often, as opposed to dipping into it occasionally.*

A light for dark paths

The Christian life takes most of us into situations where God's way is far from obvious. Besides, we are travelling through a world which the Bible says is 'in darkness' because its affairs are not illuminated by the life and light of Jesus.

So the Bible helps to shed light on things. It explains why people are awkward, why evil exists and how it can be overcome or avoided.

Through our regular reading of it, God will often provide us with just the illumination we need to cope with a situation or to answer a difficult question.

To think about *What would you say to someone who says they get no help from the Bible at all?*

BIBLE CHECK
Equipment for the journey: Psalm 119:97–104; 1 Peter 2:1–3
A light for dark paths: Psalm 119:105–112, 130; 1 John 1:5–7

A sword for hard battles

Paul the apostle called God's Word the 'sword of the Spirit' (Ephesians 6:17). This is because it has a sharp, powerful action. It penetrates beneath the protective layers of pride, selfishness and deceit which people sometimes use to keep God's truth out of their lives.

Sometimes we need to use the Bible like a sword, to cut down opposition to Jesus. When arguments with non-Christian friends fail, the Bible will sometimes succeed in convincing them – but we have to learn to use it carefully, not clumsily.

And when we face temptation, the words of Scripture read, spoken and applied, can help us to victory over Satan.

To think about *How can you learn how to use the 'sword of the Spirit' effectively?*

Strength to keep going

The Christian life is like a long expedition through different kinds of country. Sometimes the going is quite easy, like walking on level ground.

At other times it is hard, like climbing a steep rocky hill or struggling through a fast-flowing river or dense forest. It is then that Christians can become disheartened.

The Bible provides encouragement and strength to keep going. Sometimes the hardest thing to do is actually to open the Bible; the devil does all he can to make us doubt its power and so stop us using it.

To think about *What are your favourite Bible passages? Discuss how they can help sustain you at difficult times.*

Postscript *The Bible does not group together all its teaching about specific issues. To find out what it says, we need to get to know it well.*

A sword for hard battles: Psalm 119:9–11, 113–115; Ephesians 6:17; Hebrews 4:12,13
Strength to keep going: Psalm 119:25–40; 73–80; 2 Timothy 2:15

BIBLE SUMMARY

Jesus' view of the Bible

Jesus, although he was the Son of God who came to reveal God's truth to mankind (Hebrews 1:1–4), used the Bible of his day, the Old Testament, a great deal.

A weapon to fight with

When he was confronted by the devil in the desert before he began his public ministry, Jesus answered his temptations by quoting the Bible (Matthew 4:1–11). He found in Scripture a perfect and simple answer to his temptations. He did not argue; he just showed what God's Word said, and stood by it.

Evidence of God's work

Frequently Jesus, and the apostles, quoted the Old Testament to show how events in their experience had been foretold, and to prove that God was still at work. For example, he said John the Baptist was the prophet foretold several centuries earlier by Malachi (Matthew 11:10). And he applied the Bible to those who refused to listen to what he said. As the prophets had warned, they had refused to listen just when God was trying to speak to them in a new way (Matthew 13:14,15).

Support for his actions

Jesus was often challenged by people to justify what he was doing, especially when it conflicted with their customs. So, when he was accused of breaking the Old Testament law about observing the sabbath, he quoted a precedent, the action of King David, for what he was doing (Matthew 12:1–8).

To think and pray about *What steps are you taking to get to know God's Word better?*

SHARING WITH A BLIND MAN (Adrian Neilson)
Not only are we to let God's word shape what we believe, but we are also to share it with those in need.

HANDLING GOD'S WORD

The key truth *To discover the truth of God's Word, we need to approach it in several different ways.*

Reading it regularly

Most Christians find it helpful to spend some time each day reading the Bible, usually just before their prayer time, perhaps first thing in the morning or last thing at night.

This helps to focus our thoughts on God and gives us subjects to pray about. Some lesson from the Bible can be used as a basis for prayer for ourselves or others, or for worship and praise.

Using the Bible in this way, we can read steadily right through it. It is easiest to start with one of the Gospels, say, Mark, then move on to some of Paul's letters (Ephesians is a good one to begin with), before turning to the Psalms in the Old Testament. That way, we get a broad taste of the different parts of the Bible.

To think about *'Open your Word to my heart, and my heart to your Word'. What are the conditions for helpful Bible reading?*

Soaking it up

In countries where there are few books, or where many people are unable to read, God's Word has always been memorised. The habit of learning passages by heart is a good one, even for those who have a Bible readily available.

There are two reasons for this. One is that, like Jesus, we then have an instant reply to the devil's temptations. We can answer him back quickly and decisively.

The other is that we will know exactly what we believe at any time of need. A few basic verses such as John 3:16 will remind us of the basic gospel, and promises such as Matthew 11:28 will help us when we are under pressure.

BIBLE CHECK
Reading it regularly: Joshua 1:8; Psalm 119:97; 1 Peter 2:2; 2 Timothy 3:16,17

To think about *Recall a verse which you remember for a special reason. Then learn another!*

Studying its teachings

There is much to learn from the Bible about God, the world, ourselves, and what Jesus has done and will do for us.

So in reading the Bible, we also need to fit together the teachings we get from its different parts. Then we can build up a picture of God's truth, and will not be prey to false teachers who try to unsettle our faith.

If you have a Bible with cross-references in the margin, or if you have a concordance, you can follow through a subject more easily. If not, make some notes as you go along and build up your own index of subjects. There are also some helpful books on Bible teaching available.

To think about *Why do some people introduce false teaching into the church?*

Discovering its characters

The Bible has many rich descriptions and accounts of people who learned the hard way to do God's will.

It is thrilling to know some of them, like the young shepherd who became King David. Others are tragic figures, like Samson, full of physical strength and courage, but morally weak. Yet all of them have both achievements and failures.

They have much to teach us, because we see ourselves and others in them. Time spent gathering together the stories about such people from the different Bible books in which they appear can be rewarding and enjoyable.

To think about *Who is your favourite Bible character, and why?*

Postscript *When you come to a 'difficult' passage in God's word, try to interpret it in the light of other related statements in the Bible in which the meaning is clear. The obvious, most simple explanation is usually the right one.*

Soaking it up: Psalm 119:11; James 1:22–25
Studying its teachings: Matthew 7:15–23; 1 Timothy 4:6–10; 6:3–5
Discovering its characters: Hebrews 11:24–28; 12:1–3

BIBLE SUMMARY

Understanding God's Word

Some people have claimed that you can make the Bible say what you want it to. That is true, if you take statements or sentences out of their context. There are three things to ask about any passage which will help you understand it. Take as an example the parable of the Good Samaritan in Luke 10:25–37.

What sort of passage?

This is clearly not an historical event, nor is it a closely argued piece of Christian doctrine. It is a parable, a story designed to teach one point. Jesus shows this at the end (vs.36,37). It is a story which was, of course, quite plausible. Something like it probably had happened.

What does it say?

The main elements are that first and foremost we must love God (vs.25–28) but that loving our neighbour goes hand in hand with it as an expression of that love. And our neighbour can be anyone in need, not just someone we happen to like – Jews did not like Samaritans.

What does it mean for me?

Jesus' command to the lawyer (v.37) is always applicable. This is not a nice story to be enjoyed, but an example to be applied.

To think and pray about *Take another passage, say one of Jesus' miracles, and ask the above questions about it. And if you want some help for Bible reading, contact the Scripture Union (130 City Road, London EC1V 2NJ) who will send you details of the notes they have available.*

Belonging

The deepest longing and cry of the human heart is to belong.
Not to be needed or wanted is a burden few can bear. This
is why loneliness should not be tolerated in the community
of God's people.
Belonging as Christians is to be a real and lasting experience
because . . .

We belong to God's family;
We belong to each other
in worship, in sharing, in unity,
in practical ways, and in witness.

TOWARDS THE MATTERHORN (Adrian Neilson)

BELONGING TO GOD'S FAMILY

The key truth *All Christians are members of God's international family, the church, because of their shared faith in Christ.*

One Father

There is only one God. Despite all the different religions and different ideas about him, only one God truly exists. And he, says the Bible, so loved the world that he sent his Son Jesus Christ into it so that we could be reunited with him.

God becomes our 'Father' in a special way when we receive the risen, living Lord Jesus into our hearts and homes, giving them over to his control.

And he is 'Father' to all Christians, everywhere. Because we belong to him, we also belong to one great 'family', his church.

To think about *A good father cares for his children. List the ways in which God the Father cares for us.*

One Lord

Christians are not only worshippers of the one true God. They are servants of Jesus Christ, too.

Jesus was unique. While being fully human, though sinless – his physical needs and emotional feelings were like ours – he was also fully God. Through him, God took on the limitations of human life in order to reveal himself to us and to bring us back to himself.

That is why the Bible calls Jesus 'Lord', a title it usually reserves for God. Jesus is king over the whole world, and he becomes our king, or Lord, when we first trust him. All Christians share this relationship with him.

To think about *Consider all the sacrifices Jesus made when*

BIBLE CHECK
One Father: Acts 17:22–31; Romans 1:18–23; 1 John 3:1

he came to this world as a man. What does this imply for our relationship to him?

One Spirit

The Christian church was 'born' when God sent his Holy Spirit on the first followers of Jesus. It was six weeks after Jesus' final resurrection appearance (his 'ascension'), on the Jewish festival of Pentecost.

The Holy Spirit is active in every Christian: we could not even have come to trust Jesus without the Holy Spirit first showing us our need of him.

So he binds us together in one family. He is the invisible bond who creates unity and friendship between Christians. He gives us 'gifts' or talents to help each other grow in faith.

To think about *What steps can we take to 'keep the unity of the Spirit through the bond of peace' among Christians?*

One faith

Christians differ widely from one another not only in personality but also in the aspects of the faith they emphasise, and in the ways they express it.

But there is really only one Christian faith. It is summed up in the basic truths which all members of God's family share, and which centre on what Jesus did for us.

He became a man, died so that our sins could be forgiven, rose from the dead, and now promises eternal life to all who trust him. And those who teach differently, says the Bible, do not belong to the family.

To think about *How would you answer the person who says that it does not matter what you believe so long as you lead a good life?*

Postscript *It is important to distinguish between those truths which are essential to genuine Christian faith, and those which, while important, can be interpreted and applied in different ways. Christian unity is based on the former, not the latter.*

One Lord: John 8:51–59; Philippians 2:5–11
One Spirit: Acts 1:1–5; 2:1–4; Ephesians 4:1–7
One faith: 1 Corinthians 15:1–8; Galatians 1:3–9

BIBLE SUMMARY

All one in Christ

Christianity is the only faith or ideal which has consistently achieved what all others seek: genuine unity and equality of people while continuing to respect and value their different abilities.

Rich and poor

The first Christians came from a variety of backgrounds. Many were poor and uneducated, working as slaves (1 Corinthians 1:26–29). But some came from the rich and ruling families (Philippians 4:22), and others were evidently well-off householders who gladly opened their homes as meeting places for the church (Romans 16:3–5).

Jew and Gentile

Perhaps the greatest miracle in the early church was the discovery by the first believers, who were Jews, that God's purposes in Jesus included non-Jews (Gentiles) as well (Acts 10:9–16, 34–38).

They met to discuss this, and decided that no Jewish customs should be imposed on others (Acts 15:12–21). Later, Paul was to describe how God had broken down the wall of hostility between the groups, something men, not God, had erected (Ephesians 2:11–22).

No distinction

The church knows no sexual, social, racial or cultural *barriers* (Galatians 3:28). But such *distinctions* have not been destroyed; so everyone retains his personal identity. Our differences have been put into perspective by something greater: the love of Jesus for all who know they are sinful and need his forgiveness and new life (Colossians 1:15–23).

To think and pray about *What barriers between people need the healing, reconciling work of Jesus in your community?*

HAPPY NIGERIAN GIRL (Peter Heaps)
One of the joys of the Christian faith is that it does not raise barriers which prevent people from embracing it.

BELONGING TO EACH OTHER

The key truth *Because Christians all belong to God's family, there is a special bond of love between them.*

Baptised into Christ

The one thing above all others which binds Christians together is the fact that we all have to start the Christian life at the same place – the cross of Jesus Christ.

For there, man and God were reconciled. From the cross comes the possibility of new, eternal life. Jesus' death shows that we all have the same basic need: we are all sinful, and we need his 'salvation'.

Baptism, in whatever form it takes, is a symbol of our submission to Jesus Christ through faith in him as our personal Saviour. Being put under, or sprinkled with, water, symbolises death to our old self; rising from the water signifies the new life the risen Jesus gives; the water itself is a sign of the washing away of our sins. By entering God's family in the same way – through faith – we are united to each other.

To think about *Paul often uses the phrase 'in Christ' to describe the Christian's status. What do you think he means?*

A club for sinners

Sometimes the church is made out to be an exclusive club for good people. In fact, it is just the opposite. It is where people meet who know they are not good, and who need the help of Jesus.

Every Christian already belongs to the family of God, so it is a natural thing to join with others to share our faith, encourage and help each other, and worship God together.

Each person will find some churches more helpful than others. Try to find one where the Bible is clearly taught and believed, and where the people are wanting to learn and grow together.

BIBLE CHECK
Baptised into Christ: Romans 3:21–26; Galatians 3:23–28

To think about *There are many kinds of people in the church, some of whom we may not naturally like. How then can we begin to work and worship together?*

A new set of friends

When some people become Christians, their old friends (or even relatives) do not want to know them any more. And even if they do, they may not understand their new approach to life.

Within the church, however, will be people whom we can learn to love and trust. They will be able to help us – and we may be able to help them.

Making new friends takes time. It calls for openness and tact by all concerned. But because you already have the bond of faith, do not wait for others to approach you first!

To think about *'Love is patient . . . kind. It does not envy, it does not boast, it is not proud. It is not rude, it is not self-seeking . . .' How can this ideal become real in the church?*

En route for heaven

There is a good answer to those who say it does not matter if Christians don't get on with each other. We will have to get on with each other, in heaven!

Jesus has promised us eternal life. In heaven, which is the visible presence of God, the whole church is gathered together to worship and praise Jesus.

Therefore he wants us to make every effort to express and enjoy our oneness on earth. Besides, if the world sees our love for each other, it will be encouraged to take our message seriously.

To think about *How can we help our churches to become a little more like glimpses of heaven?*

Postscript *We should never expect a local church to be perfect – because no single member of it is perfect. And we should expect to find needy people in it, who find only in Jesus the answer to their needs.*

A club for sinners: Ephesians 2:1–7; Hebrews 10:23–25
A new set of friends: Romans 16:1–16; 2 Timothy 4:11–22
En route for heaven: Revelation 7:9–14; John 13:35

BIBLE SUMMARY

A universal church

The church of Jesus Christ does not consist of man-made structures or 'denominations', so far as God is concerned. So no single group can claim to be 'the one true church'. The real church is made up of people throughout the world who have submitted their lives to Jesus' control. Jesus cares for and develops their relationship with one another (Ephesians 5:25–27).

Different in emphasis

The differences in human personality are not eliminated by faith in Jesus. They are not meant to be. But they have led to churches which cater for a certain kind of person, which emphasise certain doctrines more than others, or which worship in a certain kind of way.

Paul condemned divisions in the church at Corinth (1 Corinthians 1:10–13), but he did not insist that the separate groups always met together or did everything in the same way. *Differences* are allowed in the Bible, but *divisions* are not.

United in truth

The New Testament knows nothing of close-knit international 'churches'. It only knows of a loose federation of local churches, which are joined together by mutual love and concern, and kept in touch with each other by the apostles and other teachers.

What united them was their concern for the truth of the gospel (Philippians 1:3–11). Christians who are agreed on the basic truths of the gospel are able to witness powerfully together in their community, even if they worship in different buildings.

To think and pray about *How would you define true Christian unity, and how would you express it?*

SEE-THROUGH GLOBE (Robert F. Hicks)
As Christians we belong to a universal church. Although we come from different countries and cultures, with different characteristics and levels of experience, we are all still 'one in Christ Jesus'.

WORSHIPPING TOGETHER

The key truth *Worship is a natural expression of a Christian's love for God; sharing with others in worship can stimulate our faith.*

The reason for worship

'God is worthy to be praised!' That is what the writers of the Psalms – which are like hymns – conclude.

There are many aspects of God's character which inspire worship. He made, and continues to uphold, the physical universe. He loves, cares and provides for his people. He sent Jesus to die on the cross for our sins. He promises to bring justice and peace to the new world he will make when Jesus returns to earth.

These things give the Christian a sense of thankfulness for his goodness, and wonder at his greatness. They are the basis for Christian worship.

To think about *What are you specially conscious of at the moment, for which you can worship God?*

The object of worship

Every human being needs to worship someone or something outside themselves. That is part of being made in the image of God: he has built into human nature the need to worship him.

Worship is simply concentrating our whole mind, heart and life on something in which we find satisfaction. So in some places people build statues to please the spirits which they believe will help or hinder their life.

Elsewhere, people devote themselves to jobs, political ideals, pastimes, and so on. But for the Christian, Jesus, the Father and the Holy Spirit alone are worthy of

BIBLE CHECK
The reason for worship: Psalm 147:1–11; 150:1–6

worship. They alone hold everything together and give meaning and purpose to life.

To think about *What do people in your community put in the place of God as an object of worship?*

The source of worship

There are times when we feel more like worshipping God than at others. We may be conscious of some special help he has given us, or, by contrast, we may be anxious about something.

But Christian worship is not dependent on our feelings. It focuses on God who never changes.

And it is inspired at all times by the Holy Spirit within us. He alone can lift our hearts to God. Otherwise we could easily become self-satisfied or depressed.

To think about *How can you ensure that in a church service you worship 'in the Spirit', and not just as a routine?*

The value of worship

Worship has three important effects. The first is that it reminds us of how great God is. We need that reminder because daily events can blind us to him, just as a small object in front of our eyes blocks out the sun.

Secondly, it lifts our spirits. It can restore to us the joy of knowing Jesus, even when we find life difficult. Worship with other people can be very stirring.

And finally, it can open us to the power of God. He loves a cheerful giver, the Bible says; if we give ourselves in whole-hearted worship, we are more ready to receive his gifts of love.

To think about *Discuss the relative values of worship on one's own, and with other Christians.*

Postscript *There are many styles of worship. We need to find a church whose worship style suits our personality, and where we can feel part of God's family.*

The object of worship: Romans 1:20–23; Revelation 4:8–11
The source of worship: Ephesians 5:18–20; Philippians 3:3
The value of worship: Psalm 96; Acts 16:25–34

BIBLE SUMMARY

Make a joyful noise!
There are many elements in Christian worship. It is helpful to use all of them, in private as well as in church.

The need for order
Most churches have a structure for their worship. People often find this helpful, because they know what is happening all the time. Paul stressed the need for order, but he also allowed for spontaneous contributions as the Holy Spirit prompted them.

God, he said, is 'not a God of disorder but of peace' and people should be helped (or 'edified') in worship, not confused. (1 Corinthians 14:26,33,40).

Songs and silence
Music has always been a vital ingredient in worship (see Psalm 150). A catchy tune and stirring words can unite people in praise, perhaps with hand-clapping (Psalm 47:1; James 5:13), and a quieter, moving hymn can strike a note of wonder.

But silence is helpful, too, when we can sit and remember God's presence with us, think about a passage from the Bible or something which has just been said, and 'listen' for God to teach us through it (Psalm 62:1; Ecclesiastes 3:7; Zechariah 2:13).

Body, mind and spirit
Every part of our personality can be used in worship of God. He looks for whole-hearted love and service, rather than outward ceremonies which can sometimes be meaningless (Amos 5:21–24; Romans 12:1,2).

In Bible times, people used to stand up to pray, sometimes lifting their arms into the air (Psalm 141:2; Luke 18:10–14). It does not matter what position we take up, so long as God is really worshipped.

To think and pray about *What can you do to make your own worship more helpful and meaningful?*

SCHOOL ASSEMBLY (Gordon Gray)
The fellowship of worshipping together in reverence, joy and freedom will for most of us be a means of renewing our determination to live for Jesus in our daily lives.

SHARING TOGETHER

The key truth *Worship in church meetings is a time not only for meeting with God, but also for sharing with each other in 'fellowship'.*

Praying together

When we meet with other Christians to worship God, it is easy to treat the meeting as if it were our own personal time of worship or prayer which we have when other people happen to be having theirs.

Worship together, however, is really a time when the whole family of God brings its joint praises and requests to the Father.

Coming to the Father with things we are all agreed about can be a powerful way of drawing still closer to each other in love and unity. And God has made a special promise to answer our prayers when we are united in our requests.

To think about *What things should you and your Christian friends be specially agreeing on and praying about?*

Learning together

The Bible is, under the guidance of the Holy Spirit, an open book. Anyone can read and understand it. At least, they can do so up to a point. But God has appointed some members of his family to be teachers so that we can understand its truth more adequately.

Such people have a special gift of understanding, explaining and applying God's word. Through their ministry the rest of us can grow closer to God and serve him more effectively.

It is therefore helpful to listen to, or read, their teaching. But it is also helpful to meet in groups to discuss each other's insights into the Bible and how we can apply it locally.

To think about *How would you answer someone who said*

BIBLE CHECK
Praying together: Matthew 18:18–20; Acts 4:31; 12:6–12
Learning together: Acts 2:42; 1 Timothy 4:13

that he preferred a simple faith and was afraid of being confused by other people's teaching?

Giving together

Part of our worship of God is giving gifts of money or goods to those who work in the church full-time to teach us and to win others for Jesus. Gifts for other members of the family of God who may be in special need are important, too.

In some churches, the collection of gifts, or the 'offertory', is part of the worship service. In others, a container for gifts is placed by the door. And some people prefer to give directly to the people or church agencies of their choice.

There are no set rules about how much to give. But many Christians find that the Old Testament standard of one-tenth of their income is a helpful one to follow.

To think about *What should be our attitude to giving in view of the fact that Jesus gave everything for us?*

Eating together

The night before he was crucified, Jesus had a meal with his closest friends. During that meal he took a loaf of bread, broke it into pieces and passed it round. Then he passed round a cup of wine for all to drink.

He said that those two staple food items symbolised his broken body and shed blood on the cross, through which we can be reconciled to God.

Ever since, the 'breaking of bread', 'holy communion' or 'eucharist', has been central in the worship of Christians. By eating bread and drinking wine together, we recall all that Jesus has done for us. That physical act is a powerful reminder of our unity with him.

To think about *Why do you think churches are very careful about who they allow to share in holy communion? Who is it really for?*

Postscript *Sharing together also includes sharing our joys and sadnesses with those who can appreciate them and who will pray or rejoice with us.*

Giving together: Malachi 3:8–12; Acts 4:32–37; 1 Corinthians 16:1,2

Eating together: Matthew 26:26–29; 1 Corinthians 11:23–32

BIBLE SUMMARY

One in fellowship
'Fellowship' is a biblical word which means 'sharing together'. The original word, *Koinonia,* is sometimes used because it is well known. It sums up the love and concern we are encouraged to show to each other.

Centred in Jesus
If we trust him and live as he wants us to, said Jesus' closest friend, John, we have fellowship with him (1 John 1:2–7). This is the basis for fellowship with other Christians. It reminds us of the incredible fact that we are Jesus' friends, and not just servants (John 15:14,15).

Sharing together in Jesus
Our fellowship with each other is therefore a loving expression of gratitude that God has drawn us to himself (1 Corinthians 1:9,10). It is shown in our caring for one another's needs (1 John 3:14–18), by being sensitive to and sharing in one another's joys and sorrows (Romans 12:15), and loving in the same self-giving way as Jesus loved us (John 13:34).

To think and pray about *How can you express your fellowship more openly with other Christians?*

CROSS OVERLOOKING SANTA BARBARA MISSION (Robert F. Hicks)
The cross of Christ is a constant reminder to all Christians that our fellowship is to be a loving, giving, caring community, reflecting Jesus in thought, word and deed.

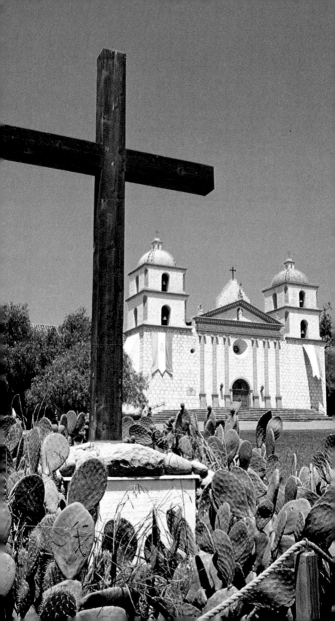

MINISTRIES FOR EACH OTHER

The key truth *God has provided a number of different functions or 'ministries' within the church so that it can grow and work smoothly.*

The need for leaders

Jesus once looked at the crowds of people who followed him everywhere, and felt sorry for them. He said that they reminded him of sheep without a shepherd. They appeared aimless and confused.

Throughout history, God has always provided leaders who can see where God wants his people to go, and who are able to encourage and inspire them to follow.

That does not mean they have the authority to push people around, however. But there is both a human and spiritual need for people with genuine vision and God-given enthusiasm and confidence who will act as responsible leaders. Otherwise, we might do nothing at all for him.

To think about *What are the qualities you would look for in a leader in your church?*

The need for pastors and teachers

A pastor is one who is able to help people in a personal way; a teacher is one who can explain the truths of Christianity clearly. Sometimes, but not always, the same person has both gifts.

We need people who are able to help or 'counsel' us because everyone faces problems or difficult situations from time to time. The pastor's advice should be based on the Bible, and coupled with deep human and spiritual insight.

The need for teachers is that we may grow in the faith and avoid errors of belief, which will weaken our effectiveness for God. We can never learn enough about him, but such knowledge will strengthen our faith.

BIBLE CHECK
The need for leaders: Matthew 9:35–38; Joshua 1:1–6
The need for pastors and teachers: 1 Timothy 4:11–16;

To think about *How much do you think we should all share in pastoral and teaching activities?*

The need for organisers

During the first exciting months of the Christian church, after the Day of Pentecost, the twelve apostles found they were doing everything: preaching, teaching, counselling, organising meetings and distributing gifts.

They felt this was wrong, so they appointed some 'deacons'. They were strong Christians and had a gift for organising things and handling money. They took over the practical work, leaving the apostles to do their own work unhindered.

There will always be people to do this today, to save the church minister from becoming overworked.

To think about *Why are practical tasks important in the church?*

The need for submission

The leader, the pastor, the teacher, and others with different gifts, such as prophets and evangelists, can only exercise their ministries if the rest of the church allows them.

Paul said that when people claim to speak God's word, we should test what they say by the scriptures, and think it over. But if we have already acknowledged their gifts, then it is natural for us normally to submit to their judgement.

Otherwise, chaos will ensue. God told the prophet Ezekiel that people would praise his words but not apply them. They refused to follow God's leading through the prophet, and so their witness became weak and ineffective.

To think about *How can we balance submission and personal independence?*

Postscript *The church is neither a dictatorship, with one person making all the decisions, nor a democracy, where everyone takes part in decision making. Rather, it is a fellowship, with all sharing as God enables them.*

---

2 Timothy 4:1–5
The need for organisers: Acts 6:1–7; Romans 12:6–8
The need for submission: Ezekiel 33:30–33; 1 Corinthians 14:29; Hebrews 13:17

BIBLE SUMMARY

Ministry in the New Testament

The main emphasis in the early church was that every Christian had some ministry which others could benefit from (Romans 12:4–6). There is no such thing as a one-man ministry in the New Testament, with a single person trying to do everything. But there are certain leadership functions outlined.

Apostles and prophets

The apostles had unique authority from God to establish churches and teach the truth (Romans 1:1; 1 Timothy 2:7). Prophets were often used to bring a direct word from God to the people (Acts 11:27–30). Christians today are not agreed on exactly how, or even if, the equivalent of the first apostles and prophets exists.

Elders or bishops

It would seem as if each church had several elders (the Greek word is sometimes translated 'bishop') who were the 'shepherds' or 'overseers' of the church. They were the local leaders, who encouraged the church, and probably often acted as teachers as well. Paul describes such people in 1 Timothy 3:1–7.

Deacons and other organisers

Paul also describes deacons, in 1 Timothy 3:8–13. It is clear that he expected those who took any responsibility to be people others respect (compare Jesus' statement in Luke 12:48).

Other ministries in the church included helpers, who assisted in practical tasks (Romans 12:7); people with the gift of healing (1 Corinthians 12:9); some who could speak or interpret other languages inspired by God in worship or prayer (1 Corinthians 12:10); and those who performed acts of mercy or kindness (Romans 12:8).

To think and pray about *What gifts has God given you and your friends to contribute to the church fellowship?*

SHEPHERD WITH HIS SHEEP (Alan Hayward)
The Bible picture of shepherds as leaders in Christ's church gives us a sense of the genuine care and service they have for God's people. All positions of leadership are both a privilege and a responsibility.

WORKING TOGETHER

The key truth *The church is often called 'the body of Christ', because like a body it consists of many parts all working together for the good of the whole.*

The local church

The church of Jesus Christ exists on three levels. There is the worldwide church of all true believers, which does not have a single, recognisable structure. Then there is the regional or national church, which may have its own customs.

And there is the local church, to which we belong. That local expression of 'the body of Christ' is truly Jesus' hands, feet and voice in the local community, taking his love and message to those who need it.

Most local churches function to some extent independently, although many are also linked to other churches in the 'denomination', which have a similar outlook.

To think about *What sort of things do you think a church could do to show the love of Jesus to the neighbourhood?*

A caring church

The church is more like a hospital than a hotel. Rather than offering shelter to the spiritually rich, it offers help to the spiritually poor and sick.

A church which is being faithful to Jesus will attract all kinds of people, some of whom no one else cares for. They may have personal problems, or be difficult to get on with. But Christians are told in the Bible to welcome one another in the Lord. Such care is not always easy, but it is an expression of, and response to, God's love to us.

To think about *What was it about us that caused God to*

BIBLE CHECK

The local church: Matthew 5:14–16; Revelation 2:12–17
A caring church: Matthew 5:46–48; Colossians 1:3–8

send Jesus into the world to die for us? What does that suggest about the quality of our love for one another?

A witnessing church

The good news about Jesus is too good to be kept to ourselves. Indeed, there is no other hope for human beings to find God except through Jesus.

So we also have a duty to tell others about him. That is partly an individual matter. We can share our faith, however difficult we find it to put into words, with our families and friends.

But the church as a whole also proclaims the gospel. Often it can do so more effectively than the individual because we can pool all our resources to make a united impact with our message and new life.

To think about *What are the most appropriate methods for preaching the gospel in your area?*

A growing church

The church, like a human family, is always growing. New members are being born into it. Some members leave the area and set up a new branch of the family where none existed before.

There are two sorts of growth we can expect to see. One is growth in numbers, as people become Christians and join in the life of the family.

The other is growth in holiness. Together we can look for ways in which we can come closer to Jesus as a group, and discover how we can be more effective in our witness for him. He always has something fresh for us to do and learn.

To Think about *What can we do to help prevent our churches from becoming stagnant?*

Postscript *Because the church consists of more than our own local group of Christians, we are encouraged in the Bible to learn about others and to help them whenever possible.*

A witnessing church: Matthew 28:18–20;
1 Thessalonians 1:8–10
A growing church: Acts 2:46,47; Ephesians 4:15,16

BIBLE SUMMARY

The church across the world

From its spectacular beginning in Jerusalem around the year AD 33, the Christian church spread right across the Roman Empire, westwards into Europe and eastwards towards India, by the end of the first century. Indeed, it was an international church from the beginning, because many turned to Christ from the wide variety of nationalities present in Jerusalem on the Day of Pentecost (Acts 2:7–13).

Sharing our riches

The church soon learned to share its blessings. For example, when there was a famine in Jerusalem, the churches of Asia Minor, hundreds of miles away, organised a collection and sent the money, so that their brothers and sisters in Christ would not go hungry (Acts 11:29,30; 1 Corinthians 16:1–4). Through Paul and the other apostles, news about various churches spread, so that all were encouraged (Colossians 1:3–8).

A missionary church

But above all, the church has a message for the world. Jesus has called us to go to every race, tribe and language with the gospel, so that all have an opportunity to hear it before Jesus returns to earth (Matthew 24:14; Revelation 7:9,10).

For Peter, Paul and their friends no distance was too great, no hardship too severe, to prevent them going to strange lands with the only message which can unite, save and renew men and women everywhere. Paul's example remains a challenge to this day (2 Corinthians 11:23–33).

To think about *What partnership in the gospel with overseas churches are you and your Christian friends able to make?*

Testing

The fact that all of us are tested in certain ways does not reduce its effect on our lives and reactions especially when it is for the first time and seems peculiar to ourselves.

The problems we face can be mental, emotional, physical, or spiritual. They can also be external, and over which we have little or no control.

What is more remarkable, however, is the evidence of so many who have been tested, demonstrating that . . .

Doubt can be turned to faith
Temptation can be turned to victory
Pain can be accompanied by God's grace
Persecution can lead to peace.

GLACIER ON THE WAY TO THE MATTERHORN
(Adrian Neilson)

THE REALITY OF TESTING

The key truth *Every Christian's faith is tested so that we may grow stronger.*

It happens to everyone

Think of the most famous people in the Bible: Abraham, Moses, David, Jesus, Paul. They all went through times of testing, when living for God seemed especially hard.

Sometimes they faced opposition when people tried to stop them doing God's work. Sometimes they had to battle with strong personal desires to leave God's way.

And at times it seemed that everything was against them as problems and difficulties mounted up. But they became famous, partly because they showed how to overcome the difficulties everyone faces.

To think about *Why should the Christian expect to be tested?*

It may not seem fair

When people suffer in some way, they sometimes complain that they do not deserve such an experience. They feel that God is wrongly punishing them by inflicting trouble on them.

But suffering is not usually a matter of deserved or undeserved punishment. We simply live in an imperfect world – one which has been made imperfect by generations of human sinfulness – and everyone inevitably faces problems.

Sometimes it seems that bad people get away with their sin, however, while Christians find the going very hard. That is not always true, and God promises that all sin will be punished eventually. But as Christians are opposed to evil, we can expect the devil to try hard to upset us.

BIBLE CHECK
It happens to everyone: 1 Peter 4:12–16; 5:8–11
It may not seem fair: John 16:32,33; Revelation 21:5–8

To think about *Life may not always seem fair, but we know God still loves us. What reasons do we have for saying this?*

It is allowed by God

The things which test our faith most are often those we least expect to happen. So it is easy to assume that they have taken God by surprise, too.

In fact, they have not. Nothing which happens to us is outside God's purposes. He does not, however, always stop unpleasant things happening. To do that he would have to be constantly interfering in the natural processes he has created, for example, to stop fire hurting someone.

This does not mean that God deliberately plans to hurt us. He wants us to let his love shine through to us always, and he never lets us be tested beyond the ability he gives us to cope.

To think about *'In all things God works for the good of those who love him.' Discuss ways in which you have found this to be true.*

It can teach us more about God

Everything in the Christian life can be used to draw us closer to God, and teach us more about him.

In fact, Christians sometimes find that in a time of testing they are made to realise just how far they have wandered from God, or just how great and loving he is.

Above all, it reminds us of just how weak and inadequate we are, and how much we need his help and power. We appreciate his help most when we most need it.

To think about *In what ways can God use a Christian who learns to trust him even in difficulty?*

Postscript *Although everyone desires a comfortable, trouble-free life, such an existence is not always as good for us as we imagine: it can lead to self-satisfaction and spiritual laziness.*

It is allowed by God: Romans 8:28–30; 1 Corinthians 10:13
It can teach us more about God: 1 Thessalonians 1:4–8; 1 Peter 1:6–9

BIBLE SUMMARY

The patience of Job

Job is an Old Testament character who was rich and well-respected. He was a godly man, too, who tried to pass on his faith to his children (Job 1:1–5). But then his world fell to pieces . . .

The role of Satan

The Book of Job reveals that Satan sometimes has access to God (1:6). He told God that Job worshipped him only because life was easy (1:10,11). So God gave Satan permission to test Job's faith, by attacking his possessions and family (1:12), and then, later, by making him ill (2:5–9).

Job's faith stayed firm

Job's faith had two aspects. There was his faith in God, which remained unshaken. He still trusted God even when people around him said he was mad to do so (1:20–22; 2:9,10). But he was also very upset (3:1–26), cursing the day he was born.

His friends told him he must have sinned, to bring such awful things on himself (e.g. 11:1–6). But his faith in his own integrity before God also remained firm; he knew he was not being punished, so his suffering remained a mystery to him.

Job's faith was deepened

But good as he was, and undeserved as his sufferings were, Job still had something to learn. God later revealed his true greatness to him (38:1–21, etc), and Job realised that even his strong faith had still been rather shallow (42:1–6). The story had a happy ending – Job became wealthy again – but he was wiser after his experience.

To think and pray about *Why was Job able to remain so faithful to God? What can we learn from him?*

WEATHER-WORN TREE (Robert F. Hicks)
Understanding testing is extremely difficult, especially when passing through it. We take courage in the testimony of many; how it strengthened their faith, and how they experienced God's goodness through it.

TESTING THROUGH DOUBT

The key truth *Doubt can be a means God uses to draw us nearer to him, but it can also paralyse the Christian's life if it is not dealt with.*

A touch of humility

There are two kinds of doubt. One is usually called 'scepticism'. It is the harsh unbelief of someone who does not wish to know and trust Jesus.

The other is the uncertainty which sometimes hits a Christian. It may be a lack of confidence about whether we really belong to God's family, or about God's willingness to do something in our life.

Such doubt can arise from genuine humility: we know ourselves to be sinful and do not expect God to be lenient. But such an attitude forgets the enormous love and power of the one who came not 'to call the righteous, but sinners to repentance' (Luke 5:32).

To think about *Discuss the difference between true humility and lack of trust in God's promises.*

A touch of opposition

Doubt is one of the chief causes of inaction among Christians. If we doubt whether something is right, or whether God wants us to act in a particular way, we are unlikely to go ahead.

That can be good, if the doubt is an instinctive re-action prompted by the Holy Spirit to something which is wrong or unwise. But it is bad, if the proposed action would honour God and help others.

So the devil often sows doubts in people's minds to stop them doing God's work, and to cause confusion in the church. Doubts, like weeds, stop the fruit of the Spirit from developing properly.

To think about *How can you distinguish between doubts sown by Satan and those prompted by God?*

BIBLE CHECK
A touch of humility: Luke 18:9–17; 1 Timothy 1:12–17
A touch of opposition: Matthew 13:24–30; 36–43;

A touch of faith

Doubt and faith are closer to each other than many people think. After all, faith, although firmly based on what God has said in the Bible, is not total knowledge.

Therefore faith can easily slip into doubt: the kind of uncertainty which the devil sowed in Eve's mind in the garden of Eden – 'Did God say . . .?' – grows worryingly larger.

When that happens, it is helpful to do two things. One is to recall the ways in which God has helped us or others in the past. The other is to remember the unchanging *facts* on which our faith is based: the total revelation of God's Word. His plan will never be inconsistent with this.

To think about *How would you help someone who doubts God's care for him, to return to his faith in the Lord?*

A touch of confidence

God does not always clear away our doubts as soon as we ask him. He may want us to think through our doubts, and return to faith much stronger as a result.

That process can be lonely and painful. We need the support of friends with whom we can talk things through – or to offer them our support, and try to understand them, when they have this experience.

But in the end, doubt, if it persists for a long time and grossly hinders our Christian life, may have to be labelled sin: it could be a refusal to take God at his word. If that is the case, then we need to confess the sin and accept, in faith, his forgiveness. That act of confidence will lead to many more!

To think about *What reasons do we have for believing that God will keep his word at all times?*

Postscript *Doubt can lead to faith, but it can also become an excuse for not pressing on in the Christian life, and accepting a comfortable existence in which God is unable to work powerfully.*

James 1:6–8
A touch of faith: Genesis 2:15–17; 3:1–22; John 20:24–29
A touch of confidence: 1 Timothy 1:3–7; 2 Timothy 1:11–14

BIBLE SUMMARY

The nature of faith

Jesus' friends once asked him to increase their faith. His reply was unexpected. If they had faith as small as a grain of mustard seed, he said, they could move mountains (Luke 17:5,6; Matthew 17:20).

It depends on God

The disciples had in fact asked the wrong question. Faith is not something which grows in quantity. It is not something we can possess more or less of; that would make it dependent on ourselves. Rather, our faith is in what *God* can do. So what seems 'a little' faith can achieve much, because it knows that nothing is too great for God (Genesis 18:14).

The disciples should have asked, '*Improve* our faith'. We need to learn how to trust God simply, without reservation. See Matthew 8:5–13, where a soldier recognised that Jesus needed only to utter a word of command, and his request would be granted.

It submits to his will

Jesus taught his followers to pray 'your will be done' (Matthew 6:10). God's will is always good (Romans 12:2), but he will often only work through people who trust him (Mark 6:5,6; 9:23,24). So faith requires boldness which expects God to work, and humility to ask only for that which will fit in with his purposes.

While it is often right to qualify our requests with 'if it is your will' (Matthew 26:39), such a prayer can be a veiled form of unbelief. There are many occasions when we can be sure that what we ask is God's will, and so pray with conviction and confidence! (John 14:14)

To think and pray about '*Is anything too hard for the Lord?*' *(Genesis 18:14) Why do we find it hard to believe that there is not?*

GRAND CANYON PEAKS (Robert F. Hicks)
When Jesus talked about 'moving mountains' it was not the physical obstacles he had in mind, but spiritual pride and defeatist attitudes. Christ would be victorious, and through his people the good news would be proclaimed throughout the world, no matter what the obstacles.

TESTING THROUGH TEMPTATIONS

The key truth *Every Christian faces temptations to disobey God, but the power of God is always greater than the temptation.*

An ever-present danger

Because many people do not acknowledge Jesus as their king, the world is full of temptations for the unwary Christian. The Christian life is like walking along a jungle path where there are dangers everywhere.

Some people will deliberately try to make us disobey God, telling us he won't notice, or that no harm can come from, say, some petty theft or lie.

The life-style of people around us will itself be a source of temptation, because it may blind us to God's better way of living. And of course, Satan will try to trip us up, and our own human nature will want to take the easy way out of a situation, without asking what God wants.

To think about *Discuss the chief sources of temptation in your area. What steps can you take so that such temptations do not take you by surprise?*

Sometimes our own fault

Jesus taught us to pray, 'Lead us not into temptation.' Another way of putting it would be, 'Do not let us stray into tempting situations.'

While we cannot avoid temptation altogether, we can often avoid people and places which are likely to provide a strong source of temptation to us personally.

Everyone is different, so there cannot be a set of rules covering every situation. But, for example, a person who easily gets drunk, should obviously avoid situations where he will be able or expected to drink a lot of alcohol. While God promises to help and protect us,

---

BIBLE CHECK

An ever-present danger: Luke 17:1–4; 1 John 2:15–17
Sometimes our fault: Matthew 6:13; 18:7–9; James 1:12–15

we should not expose our weaknesses unnecessarily.

To think about *How would you help someone face up honestly to his weaknesses, and alter his life as a result?*

Often subtle and cunning

Some temptations are very obvious – to disobey God, to lie, to steal – but others are more subtle.

Instead of being tempted to do something which is clearly wrong, we may be tempted to do something which is only wrong because it is not God's will for *us*, or because we are doing it from wrong motives. King David learned that when he tried to count the people of Israel – an act which stemmed from his pride.

And other temptations show up Satan's cunning even more; they may be half right. He simply tries to steer us gently off course, and so reduce our effectiveness for God.

To think about *In what ways does Satan disguise himself as 'an angel of light' today?*

Always a way out

Facing temptation is never easy; it is often a test of whether we really want to do what is right and to experience God's power, or to be self-indulgent.

Sometimes as we battle with temptation, the pressure to give in increases. Normally, however, each refusal to give in makes victory over the temptation easier.

There are times, too, when Satan seems to leave us alone after we have resisted him, only to come back with a renewed attack when he gets an opportunity.

Although God promised always to give us the ability to overcome temptation, we have to admit that sometimes we prefer the 'pleasures of sin'. Without our co-operation God's help is limited.

To think about *How can you increase your determination to do God's will and not give in to temptation?*

Postscript *Human will-power is not enough to overcome temptation. We need the Holy Spirit to strengthen our will so that we can resist temptations to sin.*

Often subtle and cunning: 1 Corinthians 6:1–6; 2 Corinthians 11:12–15
Always a way out: 1 Corinthians 10:12,13; James 4:7; 2 Peter 2:9

BIBLE SUMMARY

Jesus' temptations

Jesus was often tempted, and so understands and can help us when we are tempted (Hebrews 2:17,18). Few of his temptations are recorded, but those he experienced before he began his three-year teaching ministry are given in detail in Matthew 4:1–11.

Jesus was feeling weak

Jesus' temptations came when he was very tired and hungry, and so least able to resist (v.2). That is how Satan often attacks us; his only thought is to overthrow God's people by any means. Jesus became the object of Satan's attack because he knew how important Jesus was; he tries to crush all those who represent a threat – no matter how small – to his evil ways.

Satan twisted the Bible

Satan began by trying to make Jesus doubt his calling ('If you are the Son of God'; v.3). Then he twisted the Bible, quoting it at Jesus and telling him to apply its promises for the wrong reason – for the sake of a spectacular stunt, rather than out of obedience to God (v.6). Then he made Jesus a promise he had absolutely no power to fulfil (vs.8,9).

Jesus stood firm

Jesus responded in two ways. First, he quoted the Bible at Satan (vs.4,7,10). He did not argue: he simply faced Satan with the real truth. But he also trusted himself entirely to God at the same time. He *was* hungry, but he knew that God would provide bread for him without his having to misuse his own powers in a selfish way. He really did want to serve God only (v.10), and when Satan saw that, he left him alone for a while (v.11).

To think and pray about *How can we use Jesus' example in facing temptations today?*

ONE OF THE MANY GAMBLING STREETS IN LAS VEGAS (Robert F. Hicks)

We all too easily give in to the temptations that surround us, especially when we are weak and tired. The way of resistance is to become strong in God's Word.

TESTING THROUGH FAILURE

The key truth *Sometimes God allows us to make mistakes, so that we may learn to let him guide us in the way we should use our freedom.*

The gospel for failures

Jesus once told his followers that he did not come to call righteous people, but that he came to call sinners to turn back to God. That is why some people find the Christian faith unpleasant: they have to admit they have been wrong.

We begin the Christian life by admitting that in God's sight we are failures. We have not obeyed and loved him with all our heart.

God deals with us as we really are, not as we would prefer other people to imagine us. And that is true all through the Christian life: he wants us to be honest with him – and with each other.

To think about *Why is it important to be honest with God?*

The weakness of human nature

Despite all our good intentions and our prayers, we sometimes fail God. We give in to temptation. We fail to do something we know we should have done.

Sometimes we are just plain wrong. We are lazy or uncaring. Sometimes we are blind to the opportunity to experience God's power or show his love until it is too late.

That is because we are still weak even though God's Spirit dwells in our lives. Our human nature can still stray from God's path.

To think about *'The tongue . . . is a fire' (James 3:6).*

BIBLE CHECK
The gospel for failures: Luke 5:29–32; 1 John 1:5–10
The weakness of human nature: Romans 7:15–20; James

Discuss ways in which we can avoid the common sins of speech — hasty judgements, unkind words, and selfishness.

God's promise of success

When Nehemiah, an important official in the government of Babylon, went to see the king with an important request, he prayed for success. Later, when he was back in his native Jerusalem, helping to build up the ruined city, he kept praying that God's work would get done despite the opposition.

His is one of many examples in the Bible of people who faced difficult tasks, who prayed that God would help them overcome, and who eventually achieved what they set out to do.

Sometimes, however, God does ensure that despite our mistakes we still do what he wants. That reminds us of just how great he is!

To think about *Read the story of Jonah. What were his mistakes, and how did God overcome them?*

The gospel of new beginnings

When we do fail God, our faith in his love can be severely tested. We may feel very guilty or depressed because we know we have let him down.

While it is right that we should not take our failure lightly, we should not let it cripple our Christian life.

The promise of forgiveness with which we began the Christian life still holds true. God sets us on our way again, as we tell him that we are sorry for our failures. And he continues to give us the power of his Spirit with which to love and serve him.

To think about *What does Paul mean when he says we must consider ourselves 'dead to sin', and how should this affect our daily lives?*

Postscript *While God understands and forgives our failures, we cannot excuse them. He is always ready to help us do what is right.*

3:2–10
God's promise of success: Nehemiah 1:4–11; 4:9,15–20
The gospel of new beginnings: Romans 6:1–11; 1 John 2:1–6

BIBLE SUMMARY

The disciple who failed Jesus

The Bible is not full of success stories which seem entirely beyond our abilities. It has many accounts of ordinary people's failures, too, which help us to see that their successes were very much the result of God's work, and not their own special ability.

Full of promise

Peter, one of Jesus' closest followers, who was also called Simon, was always full of big promises. He boasted that he would never let Jesus down (Matthew 26:33–35). He was convinced that Jesus held all the answers to his need (John 6:67–69) and was the first to recognise Jesus as being the Son of God (Matthew 16:13–16).

A total let-down

Peter even tried to protect Jesus from going to the cross, not realising that it was part of his work to do so (Matthew 16:21–23; John 18:10,11). But when Jesus was put on trial, Peter was frightened.

The servants of the High Priest were talking over the day's events by a fire, when one of them recognised Peter as a follower of Jesus. Peter panicked and denied he had known Jesus (Mark 14:66–72). He soon realised his mistake, and broke down in tears of regret.

Back to normal

After his resurrection, Jesus made a point of talking specially to Peter, to encourage him and give him a new job to do (John 21:15–19). There was no word of rebuke; he understood, and knew that Peter was deeply sorry. From then on, Peter became a pioneer preacher introducing many people to Jesus (Acts 11:1–18).

To think and pray about *What can you learn from Peter's experience which is relevant for you?*

A COCKEREL (Robert G. Hunt)
'The cock crowed. The Lord . . . looked straight at Peter . . . Peter remembered . . . went outside and wept bitterly' (Luke 22:60–62). The lesson for us is not to trust in our own ability, but in God. When we fail, real repentance prepares the way for forgiveness.

TESTING THROUGH PAIN

The key truth *Suffering is a universal experience from which Christians are not always free, but through which they can still experience God's love.*

Pain in the world

In one sense, pain is a good thing: it is a warning that something is wrong in our body, or that danger, such as fire, is near.

But there is much suffering which in itself has no virtue: suffering from illnesses, accidents, and natural disasters which everyone can experience.

Some suffering stems directly from human sinfulness: murder, war, theft. Other forms of suffering occur because the whole world is imperfect. The Bible says everything has been affected by the sin of the human race.

To think about *What is the relationship between suffering and personal sin?*

Coping with suffering

It is natural to complain when we suffer: no one likes the experience, and we may feel it is unfair of God to allow it. But the first thing we have to learn is to accept that for the timebeing this is the state in which we have to serve God.

However, during our suffering, God may seem far away. It may be hard to pray; we may not be able to concentrate on the Bible.

Therefore Christians have a great responsibility to visit and help in every possible way all those who suffer.

What is more, we have the unfailing promise that Jesus is always with us even in our sufferings – and that his love never dries up. He knows from personal experience what suffering is about.

To think about *What practical things can we do for Christ-*

BIBLE CHECK
Pain in the world: Luke 13:1–5; Romans 8:18–23
Coping with suffering: 2 Corinthians 1:3–11; Hebrews

ians who are suffering, whether in our locality or further afield?

Healing is possible

Both Jesus and the apostles not only preached the gospel, they also healed the sick. There is no record that they healed everyone, and Paul, for example, appears to have had a long-standing problem which God did not remove (see next page).

There are two ways in which God heals people today. One is through normal medical treatment – because he is still the Lord of our bodies and their functions. And the other is as an answer to special prayer on our behalf, with or without medical treatment.

We are told to pray for healing. But healing may not always be sudden; God may have a lot to teach us as we slowly get better. The inner healing of mind and spirit is as vital as that of the body.

To think about *Discuss the possible reasons why the 'ministry of healing' is less prominent in today's church than it was in the early church.*

The end of all suffering

The Bible paints a beautiful picture of heaven, the place where all Christians will spend their lives after death in the close presence of Jesus.

In heaven, it says, there will be no more death, disease, hatred, war or any other suffering. Everything will be made new and perfect.

It is a picture which is meant to encourage and inspire us in this life. We know that one day all that we long for will happen. Meanwhile, we are not to stop our efforts to ease or remove suffering. Part of being a Christian is to bring a touch of heaven to earth.

To think about *Why does God not bring in this new age now?*

Postscript *Sometimes, it is only through suffering that the deep things of God become clear to us, and the work which God has given us to do is completed – just as Jesus had to suffer in order to do his work.*

12:7–11
Healing is possible: Mark 1:32–34; Acts 5:14–16; James 5:14,15
The end of all suffering: Romans 8:18; Revelation 21:1–4

BIBLE SUMMARY

Paul's 'thorn in the flesh'

Paul was a remarkable person. He, above all others, spelt out Jesus' teaching in detail for the benefit of the church. He travelled thousands of miles in sailing ships, on horseback and on foot to take the message of Jesus to new countries or districts.

A life of suffering

In doing that task Paul suffered a great deal. He lists some of his sufferings in 2 Corinthians 11:23–33 as he uses his experience to prove his genuineness. No one would be shipwrecked, beaten up, robbed, starved and overworked unless he believed in his calling!

Paul also wrote that he was prepared to suffer for Jesus, because Jesus had suffered much for him. He remembered, too, how he made Jesus' followers suffer before he became a Christian (Philippians 3:7–11).

Weakness becomes strength

There was, however, one particular pain from which Paul wanted to escape. He had what he called a 'thorn in the flesh' (2 Corinthians 12:7–10). No one is sure what this was. It may have been a physical deformity or very poor eyesight.

Paul felt that it hindered his work, so he prayed for healing. But God answered, 'My grace is sufficient for you, for my power is made perfect in weakness.'

Three times Paul prayed for healing, and each time God gave him the same answer. After that, he accepted his disability. He was more open than ever to receiving God's strength for his work and he proved that God could use weak people to do his will (1 Corinthians 1:25).

To think and pray about *What similar thorns do some people have today? How could we come to terms with such problems?*

CACTUS, ARIZONA DESERT, USA (Robert F. Hicks)
Paul in the footsteps of his master was called to 'suffer many things', as well as his own 'thorn in the flesh'. Remarkably, he states that through this he experienced God's power and grace; a truth that many have discussed down the ages.

TESTING THROUGH PERSECUTION

The key truth *In every generation some Christians are ridiculed, hurt or even killed by other people simply because they love and serve Jesus Christ.*

The gospel offends people

The message of Jesus brings truth to light, but some people prefer their world of lies and wrongdoing. They therefore try to stop the spread of the Christian faith or hinder Christians from living it out.

Others will ridicule the faith because its simple message seems nonsense to them. They do not believe there is a God, or if there is, they claim he has not revealed himself finally and completely through Jesus Christ.

In some countries, people regard Christianity as a threat to their political ideals, so they pass laws limiting its activities, or banning it altogether.

To think about *Discuss precisely what it is that people in your society find objectionable in Christianity.*

The ways they attack

Sometimes, the pressure on us will come from those closest to us – our families or special friends. They may have a different faith, or simply not understand what has happened to us. They may accuse us of being disloyal to them; some Christians have been thrown out of their families as a result.

Persecution can be violent. Christians have been imprisoned and tortured for their faith. They have been banned from certain jobs, or banished to special hospitals.

But often the pressure is less obvious. People may just pick arguments, or try to make us sin. They may exclude us from certain social circles, or just laugh at our faith.

BIBLE CHECK
The gospel offends people: John 15:18–27; 1 Corinthians 1:20–25

To think about *What are the most likely sources of persecution today, and how would you prepare yourself to face them?*

The call to be faithful

The taunt which Satan made against Job was that he would do anything to save his own skin. In fact that was not true, and Job remained faithful to God despite his suffering.

The threat of persecution can be more frightening than any other suffering, but the apostles and many Christians since have shown that it is just as possible to remain faithful to God under these conditions.

God wants us to remain faithful to him, even if that means not doing what other people want. He promises to give us wisdom to know what to do, and has said that he is always honoured when we stand up for him.

To think about *At their first experience of persecution, the disciples ran away. Later they stood firm. What made the difference?*

Resisting even to death

Being faithful to God meant death on the cross for Jesus. In fact, that was why he came to earth – to die for our sins.

But for some of his followers death came early, too, because they loved him. Stephen was stoned to death for sharing his vision of Jesus with the religious leaders, and became the first Christian martyr.

Ever since, people have willingly been murdered rather than deny the truth of Christianity. For most of us, it will not come to that, but the challenge to remain faithful, under pressure, right up to the moment we die, remains.

To think about *Intense persecution can be horrific to think about, but what hope and comfort does the Christian have who endures it?*

Postscript *Sometimes, Christians can bring persecution on themselves by being tactless or by making too much of secondary or less important truths.*

The ways they attack: Matthew 10:16–39; Acts 4:1–4
The call to be faithful: Acts 4:16–20; Mark 13:9–13
Resisting even to death: John 16:1–4; Acts 7:54–60; Hebrews 2:1–4

BIBLE SUMMARY

The promise of peace

'Cast all your anxiety on him because he cares for you'
(1 Peter 5:7) is one of the most memorable of the Bible's
many guide-lines. One of the strongest witnesses to the
reality of our faith is the inward peace which Jesus gives
when we obey that instruction.

A peace beyond words

Jesus promised his peace to his followers before he died
(John 14:27). He said it would be unlike anything the
world had to offer. It would not be like the temporary
release from anxiety which drugs or strong drink may
give, because they deal only with our feelings, and not
with the real problem.

Rather, his peace would be an underlying sense of
confidence that all our circumstances are in God's capa-
ble hands, and that his purposes for us are always good
even if very hard or even painful.

A peace despite trouble

The Jewish word for peace, 'shalom', means 'whole-
ness' as well as 'tranquility'. It reminds us that peace is
dependent on our relationship with Jesus. We already
have peace with God (Romans 5:1–5) in the sense that
everything which makes us his enemies has been dealt
with by Jesus' death on the cross.

So, whenever there is turmoil around us, we have an
opportunity, firstly, to experience the peace which is
the gift of God's Spirit within us (Galatians 5:22). But,
secondly, we can also use that sense of peace to help us
become peacemakers in that situation, helping others to
be reconciled to each other (Matthew 5:9).

To think about *How can our sense of peace be deepened
in us?*

Winning

Victory is something we all prefer; no one likes to be a loser. The victory we have in Christ, however, is different from the victory that the world seeks. It may seem that we lose out to the world in its quest for fame and fortune. This is because our values and ambitions are different and are not limited to time but related to eternity.

We are convinced that . . .

Victory is secured in King Jesus
Victory is experienced in our lives now
Victory effects changes in heart and life
Victory is assured over external forces
Victory gives us confidence to proclaim Christ.

SUN REFLECTED ON THE TOP OF THE MAT- TERHORN (Adrian Neilson)

JESUS IS KING

The key truth *The whole universe is already in Jesus' power, and he will one day bring all its rebellious parts to order.*

He conquered sin

'Sin' describes both the attitude and actions of people which go against God's laws and purposes. People are cut off from God by Sin.

Jesus conquered sin in two ways. First, by living a perfect life on earth he showed it was possible for people to avoid sinning and obey God.

But most of all, he conquered it through his death on the cross. There, he suffered the punishment – death itself – which each sinful person deserved, so that we could know God and receive his new life which lasts for ever.

To think about *Jesus told his followers to be perfect; just as God is perfect. How far can we expect to obey that command?*

He conquered death

'The soul who sins is the one who will die': that was the Bible's judgement until Jesus came to earth. Here more than physical death was implied: it involved spiritual separation from God.

But death could not defeat Jesus, because he was the creator of life! Although his body died completely, yet God raised him from the dead to demonstrate his total victory over the grave.

In so doing, God broke the curse which had plagued the human race for centuries. He opened up the way to heaven, so that although we, too, will have to pass through death, it cannot hold us in its clutches and keep us from everlasting life.

BIBLE CHECK
He conquered sin: Matthew 9:1–8; Romans 8:1–3; 1 Peter 2:21–25

To think about *In some places, death has become a subject no one likes to talk about. Why do you think this is so?*

He conquered evil

Because God gave every person freedom, to choose whether or not they would obey him, some people have chosen to do what is wrong. In addition, there are evil powers in the world trying to overthrow God's kingdom.

When he died on the cross, Jesus mortally wounded the forces of evil, because he conquered their ultimate weapon, death.

Now Satan is in his last days. He knows he will be totally destroyed when Jesus returns to earth. Meanwhile, he attempts to hinder God's people, but he can never harm those who trust themselves entirely to Jesus.

To think about *In what ways can we expect Satan to attack us today?*

He will conquer the world

In three of Paul's letters – Ephesians, Philippians and Colossians – he bursts into exclamations of praise at the greatness of Jesus' victory.

Jesus promises to do nothing less than conquer the whole world with his love and his truth.

He will do it in two ways. First, he will do it through his people. We are called to take and live out his message in every place. Secondly, he will do it completely when he returns to earth to create a new world in which peace, love and truth are supreme.

To think about *What are Christians to do until Jesus brings in his new world?*

Postscript *Because Jesus is king, nothing happens which he cannot use in some way for his own good purposes, even if events stem from evil sources rather than from him.*

He conquered death: Luke 24:1–9; 1 Corinthians 15:20–28
He conquered evil: Luke 13:10–17; Colossians 1:13,14; Revelation 20:7–10
He will conquer the world: Philippians 2:9,10

BIBLE SUMMARY

Jesus' cosmic plan

Sometimes, Christians talk as if God's plan to give them eternal life was simply a personal, individual matter. In fact, it has a much greater dimension. His plan includes the whole world, which he loves and cares for (John 3:16–18). It has been slowly unfolding through the years (Colossians 1:19,20).

The role of the church

The church may seem weak and powerless in the world today, but in fact it is God's new family (1 Peter 2:9). Jesus is its head, and God's new world will be filled by those who have loved and served him in this life (Ephesians 1:18–23). Those who seem great in the world will not be there, unless they too have trusted Jesus (Matthew 19:28–30; 20:1–16).

The rest of creation

The whole universe will be renewed (Ephesians 1:9,10), held together by Jesus with a new perfection and beauty. All things are out of harmony with God because of the massive impact human sin has had on the physical world. But one day everything will be reconciled to God, just as we have to believe in him (Romans 8:22; Colossians 1:19,20).

In other words, God plans a whole new creation (Revelation 22:1–5, compare 2 Corinthians 5:17–19), in which everyone will know that he is the true king, the creator of all things who alone is worthy to be worshipped and served (Revelation 4:11).

To think and pray about *What encouragement can we receive from knowing we are part of God's cosmic plan?*

VIVID SUNSET (Robert F. Hicks)
The Christian takes confidence in God's cosmic plan, not only because the church with Christ as its head plays an important role, but because goodness will triumph, the universe will be renewed, and Jesus will be acknowledged as King of kings and Lord of lords.

VICTORY IS CERTAIN

The key truth *Because Jesus has already shown his power in conquering evil and death, we can be certain of his ability to help us to honour God in every situation.*

No need to sin

We are faced with all kinds of temptations to disobey God every day. Sometimes those temptations come from our own weakness, from our circumstances, or are direct from Satan.

But whatever their source, and whatever their strength, those temptations are never more powerful than the Holy Spirit who is active in our lives. He is steadily making us more like Jesus, who resisted all temptations.

Prayer helps in overcoming temptation. We can ask God to make us more alert and sensitive, so that we see temptation coming. Also, we can pray for the Holy Spirit's power *at the time we need it:* to claim Jesus' victory over sin as our own, and to act as if we have already overcome it – and we will!

To think about *Why can we be confident that the power available to us is always greater than any opposition we face?*

No need to fear

Fear of any kind can cripple a Christian as much as a physical handicap. Like one animal being attacked by another, we may be paralysed by fear and therefore do nothing until it is too late.

But the Christian has nothing to fear, even in frightening situations, for two reasons.

First Jesus is always there, ready to help. Second, he can deal with the fears of those who love and trust him fully, so that they can serve him effectively.

BIBLE CHECK
No need to sin: Mark 11:24; Luke 11:13; 1 John 4:4
No need to fear: Psalm 34:4–6; Matthew 10:26–33;

To think about *What do people fear most in your community, and what comfort does the Bible offer them?*

No need to doubt

One of the most remarkable stories of Jesus' life was when he stayed behind while his closest followers crossed a lake in a boat. A storm blew up, and Jesus walked across the water to them.

Peter, impulsive as ever, asked if he too could walk on the water. Jesus said yes, but as soon as Peter had taken a few steps, he saw the waves and felt the wind, doubted, and began to sink.

Yet his own experience had already proved that he could walk on the water – and Jesus had told him to! Our past experience (and that of others) and Jesus' own instructions encourage us to do whatever he wants.

To think about *Discuss the kinds of situation that Jesus might lead us into where Peter's lesson and experience would be relevant.*

No need to falter

Many Christians are tested almost to breaking point. It might be constant temptation; it could be human suffering of some kind.

It is easy to grow tired, not only physically, but spiritually, too. Battling with evil can be very wearing.

But the Spirit within us will carry us through. He will give that energy we need, that extra will-power and determination to press on. God's love for us never falters, so we, too, can love and serve him consistently.

To think about *Think about ways in which you may be tempted to give in, and God's promises which will help you. Memorise some, so that you will be ready for the test when it comes.*

Postscript *There can never be any excuse for not enjoying Jesus' victory. Yet if we do fail him, we know he will not fail us, but will always forgive and renew us.*

---

2 Timothy 1:6,7
No need to doubt: Matthew 14:22–33; 21:18–22
No need to falter: Isaiah 40:27–31; Galatians 6:9; Hebrews 12:3

BIBLE SUMMARY

He is able

The New Testament is full of confidence about all that God can do. Here are some of its assertions.

Able to keep us

We know that he is able to forgive our sins and give us eternal life; Hebrews 7:25 reminds us that he is able to do this for ever. No matter what century people live in, God can save them.

And once we belong to him, he is able to keep us from falling away (Jude 24). That means victory over sin, and a certain place in heaven.

Able to help us

Jesus reminds Paul in 2 Corinthians 12:9,10 that the strength he is able to give is wholly adequate.

We experience that strength when he enables us to overcome temptation (Hebrews 2:18), and when he keeps his promises to us (Romans 4:20,21).

Able to support us

God shows his power especially by doing all kinds of things for us, through us and within us – things we often do not even expect (Ephesians 3:20,21).

He is able to provide us with whatever we need – spiritual resources and physical resources, too – so that we can do his work in his way (2 Corinthians 9:8).

To think and pray about *What in your own life or church do you need God to do specially? Which of these promises applies to that situation?*

SUNSET AND WHEAT (Robert F. Hicks)
God's daily provision for our physical and spiritual lives is to give us the strength to be involved in his work and to increase our expectation of what he can and will do, if we allow him.

RIGHT IN THE HEART

The key truth *The secret of living a successful Christian life is to ensure that our thoughts and attitudes reflect those of God.*

Jesus comes first

During his life on earth, Jesus frequently told people that if they really wanted to be his followers, he had to have first place in their lives.

Just as the Old Testament commandment said, 'You shall have no other gods before me,' so Jesus cannot fully work out his purposes for us if we value anything or anyone more highly than him.

And although that may sound a hard requirement, it is in fact the gateway to success. With Jesus first in our lives, he is free to do many great things, and we are free to enjoy them.

To think about *'The love of money is a root of all kinds of evil.' Why do you think this is?*

Thinking straight

A verse in the Book of Proverbs, which is difficult to translate, is written in one Bible version as, 'As he thinketh in his heart, so is he.' In other words, what we are like inside is what will show outwardly, however much we try to hide it. Jesus said the same thing.

Living a Christian life is not about doing certain good deeds and avoiding bad ones. It is about being in a right relationship with God, from which will come naturally certain ways of behaving.

So the Bible encourages us to let God's Spirit set our thinking straight. To help him do this, we can concentrate our thoughts on God, his goodness and his purposes.

To think about *How would you answer a person who says that it cannot really matter if you think or feel anger towards someone, as long as you do not express it outwardly?*

BIBLE CHECK

Jesus comes first: Exodus 20:3; Luke 9:23–26; 57–62; 1 Timothy 6:6–16

Pure motives

It is perfectly possible to do the right thing for the wrong reason. We can try to help someone, for example, not so much out of concern for them, but because we want to exercise power over them.

Or we can do something right in order to persuade others that we are good, unselfish people, while in fact we are just the opposite, and know it.

Ananias and Sapphira were like that in the New Testament. They sold some land and pretended to give all the money to the church, but held some back. They did not need to give it all, in fact, but the act of pretence was seen to be very serious.

To think about *Discuss the kinds of things which we can easily do with mixed or impure motives, and how we can develop true sincerity.*

Love determines action

Love for others is the golden rule of the New Testament. Our actions are to be determined by it; we are to do for others only – and everything – that we hope they would do for us.

So before doing something, it is often worth asking both what Jesus would do in the situation and what we would like done if we were on the receiving end.

But love is not soft. It sincerely desires only what will help, encourage and benefit others. Sometimes that may mean gently helping them come to terms with some sin or fault in their life or faith. Love stems from a deep and genuine concern for the other person's welfare.

To think about *What are the chief characteristics of Christian love?*

Postscript *Developing right attitudes is a good example of how we are to co-operate with God: he promises to change our attitudes, but we have to recognise where they need changing, and ask him to deal with them.*

Thinking straight: Proverbs 23:7(AV); Mark 7:14–23; Philippians 4:8
Pure motives: Acts 5:1–11; 1 Peter 2:1–3
Love determines action: Luke 6:27–36; 1 Corinthians 13

BIBLE SUMMARY

Not I, but Christ

A mistake which many Christians make is to try to live a Christian life largely by their own efforts, and only sometimes drawing on God's help. Paul's example was rather different: for him, being a Christian was to allow Jesus' life to fill and flow through him at all times (Galatians 2:20).

Many things are beyond our complete understanding, and this is one of them. 'Christ in you, the hope of glory' (Colossians 1:27), is a mystery, says Paul, but it is true just the same.

So he prays that the Christians in Ephesus may know Christ dwelling in their hearts, and so base their lives firmly on love, and begin to understand the immensity of God's purposes (Ephesians 3:14–19).

Christ changing us

When we allow Jesus to 'live through us', we are relying totally on him, but also need consciously to clear away the things which will hinder him (Ephesians 4:22–24). We are encouraged to live consistently with the new nature he has already put in us to make us like him (Colossians 3:5–17).

To think and pray about *What do we need to do in order to let Jesus fill our lives with his love?*

A LONE JOGGER (Robert F. Hicks)
We are never alone when we have Jesus, but this only becomes a real experience as we allow him to have more of us. This giving ourselves to God is a deliberate act, involving our minds, emotions and will.

OVERCOMING EVIL

The key truth *God wants his people to share practically in Jesus' conquest of evil, and to conquer it in their own experience.*

Be sure of your ground

We cannot effectively fight evil if we are unsure either about the nature of evil itself, or of the resources we can draw on.

That is why it is important to grow in our knowledge of the Bible. Through it we discover just what a Christian can believe and do, and what is untrue and wrong.

The most effective fighter in any battle is the one who has the confidence that he will never be defeated. We can have that confidence, because despite the intensity of our fight against evil, God can never be defeated – and nor need we be.

To think about *'Fight the good fight of the faith.' What is involved in this?*

Depend on God's power

With God, nothing is impossible. Furthermore, he wants to show how great and powerful he is, by doing things in our experience which we could never do ourselves in a thousand years.

In fact, the person most able to receive and enjoy God's power to overcome evil is the one who is most conscious of his need and his weakness. God is then free to work, without being hindered by our self-confidence.

Whenever we face temptation or opposition as Christians, we need to renew our trust in Jesus, rely on his promises, and receive in faith his power to speak or act wisely.

To think about *What steps can we take so that when we suddenly need God's power, we are able to receive it?*

BIBLE CHECK
Be sure of your ground: 1 Corinthians 3:10–15; 1 Timothy 6:11–16

Learn to say no

One of the problems about some kinds of sin is that they seem very attractive. They do not always appear bad. Sometimes they appeal to our natural desires for comfort or excitement.

The secret of conquering any kind of temptation is never to argue about it, or even consider it to be a possible course of action.

If we learn to say no in small things, it will be easier to stand against bigger ones. But saying no to them is only part of our saying yes to Jesus and all the far better things he offers.

To think about *Think about the Christian alternatives to evil and wrongdoing; why are they always best for us and for others?*

Tell Satan to go

Satan is sometimes like a very noisy dog. He barks loudly to frighten us away from doing God's will, but in fact if we press on in God's power, he will not be able to harm us.

Sometimes, a word of command will make him stop his activity when it is seriously endangering God's work. But we can order him to stop interfering only in the name of Jesus Christ, God's Son, praying for his authority and victory.

We must be specially careful about tangling with the forces of evil, expecially if a non-Christian appears to be controlled by them. In those cases, the way forward may be for several mature Christians to pray for that person's release from Satan's hold.

To think about *Jesus often confronted evil powers and destroyed them when he was on earth. Why can we expect him to do the same today?*

Postscript *Fighting evil is not a game, but a deadly serious business. We need not fear evil forces, but we should not belittle their strength or intentions.*

Depend on God's power: Mark 13:9–11; Luke 18:27; Philippians 4:13
Learn to say no: Matthew 16:21–23; 1 Peter 5:8,9
Tell Satan to go: Luke 10:17–20; Acts 13:4–12; 19:11–20

BIBLE SUMMARY

The armour of God

In Ephesians 6:10–20 Paul reminds his readers that the battle Christians face is not against people so much as against great armies of spiritual forces which influence many people (often without them knowing it) and which conrol many of the world's institutions and governments (v.12).

In order to deal with them effectively, he tells us to 'put on the full armour of God' (vs.11,13). Then he lists the spiritual resources we can draw on, using the picture of a Roman soldier, ready for battle.

Hold to the basics

The basic armour for the soldier was a breastplate, helmet, belt and shoes. For the Christian, our basic protection against evil is the truth of God, his righteousness, and the complete salvation Jesus gives, together with the good news which brings us peace with God and eternal life (vs.14,15,17).

Keep alert and active

In battle arrows set on fire were shot at the soldiers, who used their shields to intercept them. So, our faith is something which can be held up to deflect the dangerous arrows of temptation which will be flung at us (v.16).

We also have a 'sword' which will cut the enemy to pieces more effectively than any real weapon of war. It is the Bible, which contains God's word for every situation (v.17). And as we use these two pieces of armour, we also need to keep in touch with our commander, God, through prayer, ready to receive and obey his instructions (v.18).

To think and pray about *Discuss how you would apply Paul's teaching here in the kind of 'spiritual warfare' you are likely to meet in your everyday life.*

A DUTCH CANNON, CAPE TOWN (Bible Lands)
The history of mankind demonstrates conclusively that he is regularly in conflict with his fellow man. The Christian is also in conflict, not against people, but for people, so that God's light of truth and love might shine upon them.

RESISTING PRESSURE

The key truth *The Christian is called by God, not only to overcome any opposition, but also to resist subtle pressures which would weaken our witness.*

The pressure to conform

No one likes to be different from those around him. We all want to be considered part of a community, club or gang of friends. And so we usually adapt our behaviour to what is acceptable to that group.

But that may not always be acceptable to God. If we follow him faithfully, we shall sometimes want to be different from other people.

There is also a temptation to conform to contemporary society by not bringing the Bible to bear on every aspect of our life. So, for example, some Christians tried to prevent the abolition of slavery in the nineteenth century, simply because it was a part of the society they knew.

To think about *What are the areas in which you feel Christians should be clearly different in your community?*

The pressure to compromise

There are two dangers here. One is to water down our beliefs under the pressure of teachers or preachers who deny some important truth, or to modify our behaviour to include something which God has clearly forbidden, just because it is easier to do so.

And the other is for us to bring pressure on others by insisting that our way of doing things or our understanding of some problems is the only one possible. However, Christians do sometimes differ, in love, over secondary matters.

In the first case, we must simply stand our ground and obey God. In the second, we should obey our conscience, and learn to respect those who differ.

To think about *Compare Paul's teaching in 1 Corinthians*

BIBLE CHECK

The pressure to conform: Romans 12:1,2; Ephesians 2:1–7
The pressure to compromise: 1 Corinthians 8:7–13; 10:23–31; 1 Timothy 4:1–10

8:11–13 with 10:29,30. How can we achieve a right balance in matters of conscience?

The pressure to complain

It is always easier to complain about something or someone than to try to put matters right. It is also easy to complain against God or our church leaders when things become difficult.

The new nation of Israel complained bitterly when they had left Egypt, under the leadership of Moses, and then found themselves hungry and thirsty in the nearby desert. They had been keen enough to set off, but were not prepared to follow God through the hard ways as well as the exciting ones.

But the Christian way is always to show love, consideration and faith, rather than shout slogans. In his own kind way, Jesus tells us to get on with our business of living and serving him. We can let him be the judge of what is best for us, and of other people's actions.

To think about *What should a Christian do if he or she has a genuine cause for complaint against a fellow believer?*

The pressure of complacency

Sometimes, the Christian life is quite straightforward. There are no big problems to face, no great temptations bearing down on us.

That is just the time when we can slip into complacency. We can become content with our comfortable life and so miss all kinds of opportunities to serve Jesus, by caring for others or speaking for Jesus.

And older Christians, too, can sometimes ease up after many years of devoted service to Christ. To all comes Paul's challenge to press on.

To think about *'We have only done our duty' (Luke 17:10). Why is that in a sense not enough?*

Postscript *The example of Jesus, who loved even the unlovable people, and for whom nothing was ever too much trouble, is the one we are called to follow, even when many subtle pressures may put us off.*

The pressure to complain: Exodus 17:1–7; Matthew 18:15–22

The pressure of complacency: Psalm 121:3,4; Proverbs 6:6–11; Luke 17:7–10

BIBLE SUMMARY

United we stand

One of the functions of the church – the local group of Christians who meet together for worship and fellowship – is to help one another stand firm in the faith (Philippians 1:27,28).

That cannot happen if we are always arguing among ourselves, and the weaker brother or sister may easily slip away from God because of our neglect of their spiritual or other needs (1 Timothy 5:13–15; 2 Timothy 2:22–26).

So the New Testament is always urging us to offer support to one another, so that we may win our battles and overcome the dangers which face us as a group (1 Thessalonians 5:14).

The need for wisdom

In order to stand together on the truth of Jesus, we need to be 'wise about what is good, and innocent about what is evil' (Romans 16:17–20).

That means growing in our knowledge of how to live according to the Bible, and at the same time giving evil a wide berth (Ephesians 5:3–6).

It also means sorting out our differences swiftly and maturely, so that we can get on with our main task of proclaiming God's Word in the world (1 Corinthians 6:1–8). Jesus promised that, in united prayer, God is able to work mightily when we are all agreed (Matthew 18:19).

To think and pray about *Discuss the ways in which we can present a united face against evil.*

WATCHTOWER OVERLOOKING THE GRAND CANYON (Robert F. Hicks)
The foundation upon which the Christian builds is Christ, and one day we will have to give an account of what and how we have built. We need to be as alert as watchmen, for many enemies desire to spoil our Christian testimony.

ONWARD, CHRISTIAN SOLDIERS!

The key truth *The Christian life consists, not only in overcoming evil, but also in doing important things in the world for God.*

Building the kingdom

The 'kingdom of God' was a phrase used by Jesus to describe the extent of God's direct rule on earth over his people, and of their influence for him in the world. This kingdom is slowly growing in size and extent. Jesus said it was like a tiny seed which grows into a large shrub.

It is also growing in effectiveness. Its members are like seeds sown in good, fertile soil, said Jesus in one of his parables. Each one yields a crop of the 'fruit' of his Spirit: we each have some influence for God in our community.

To think about *Discuss the parable of the sower (Matthew 13) and put its teaching into your own words.*

Salt in the world

Salt is an important ingredient in almost everyone's diet. A small amount has a great effect.

Salt was used in Jesus' time to preserve foods like meat in order to stop them going bad when they were stored. It was also used to bring out the flavour of foods.

Jesus said that was how he wanted his people to be in the world. Our influence will help prevent human society going completely bad; God, for example, promised to hold back his judgement of Sodom in the Old Testament because of the righteous people there. And

---

BIBLE CHECK
Building the kingdom: Matthew 13:1–9; 24–32
Salt in the world: Genesis 18:26–33: Matthew 5:13; Colos-

we can bring joy and hope into the world, where they are so often lacking.

To think about *In what ways can you act as salt in your community?*

Light for the world

Light is often used in the Bible as a picture of God, because of the total contrast with sin and evil, which is often described as 'darkness'.

Jesus said he was the light of the world. He came to show up the deeds of evil people, and to make clear the way to God.

We are to reflect his light, share his love and reveal his life wherever we go. Then others will see that his ways are good and his laws right.

To think about *How do people react to God's light?*

Winning enemy territory

In human warfare, the armies not only defend themselves against each other, but also try to capture each other's land.

In the spiritual battle, God has called us to go with him into the world which is under Satan's influence, and see God himself slowly extend his kingdom.

Together with all God's people we can take the good news of eternal life in Jesus Christ to those who have never known him. We may see people who were once in Satan's grip released to serve God. We may see individuals, families and even whole communities changed by the power of God's Word.

To think about *What parts of the 'enemy territory' do you think God wants to see won for him in your area?*

Postscript *We have been told to expect to see God at work through the witness of our churches. If nothing seems to be happening it may be because we are not obeying him fully.*

---

sians 4:6
Light for the world: Matthew 5:14–16; John 1:4–13; 8:12
Winning enemy territory: Acts 8:4–8; 26–40

BIBLE SUMMARY

What is the kingdom of God?

The kingdom, or rule of God, was what Jesus came to proclaim (Matthew 4:17), and he sent his followers out to proclaim it, too (Luke 10:8,9).

His kingdom is not like a human country, however (John 18:36), and does not have any physical land. Rather, it consists of people all over the world who love and obey him (Luke 14:15–24).

Parables of the kingdom

Many of Jesus' parables were about the kingdom of God. It would grow, he said, like seed in the ground (Matthew 13:1–9, 31–32). However, there would be people who did not really belong to it but who seemed part of it (Matthew 13:36–43).

The kingdom would have a good but often unnoticed effect on the world, like yeast in a loaf of bread (Matthew 13:33). It is like a precious stone, or treasure; it is worth selling everything in order to get into it (Matthew 13:44–46).

Present and future

The kingdom of God already exists (Luke 17:20,21) wherever God's people are. But it also has a future dimension, and Jesus will establish it finally at the end of time (Matthew 25:31–40).

To think and pray about *As members of God's kingdom, how should we view the world around us?*

Serving

One of the greatest needs of the church and the world is 'committed Christians', that is, Christians who know, love and serve Jesus Christ.

This commitment is both within the church for each other, and through the church to others, both individually in our daily lives and collectively in our corporate witness. As Christians we can recognise the following . . .

Service is for all
Power to serve is for all
Fellowship involves service
Love involves service
God's good news needs sharing
Our Christian commitment is for life.

BELOW THE MATTERHORN (Adrian Neilson)

CALLED TO SERVE

The key truth *God wants every Christian to take part in his work in the world.*

Called by God

When we became Christians by asking God's forgiveness for our sins and trusting him to give us eternal life, we also became Christian workers.

God has brought us into his worldwide family of people who love him. As in every family, there are lots of jobs to be done if our lives are to run smoothly. No one is expected to be lazy and do nothing.

God has also put us in a part of the world where he wants us to show his love and spread his truth. We are called by him to be his servants, to do his will wherever we are.

To think about *What has God called each Christian to do above everything else?*

Compelled by love

The first Christians could never have been accused of being half-hearted. They were almost reckless in the way they threw themselves into their service for Jesus.

The reason was quite simple. They were so amazed at the love of God for them, that nothing was too hard or too much trouble for them to do in gratitude to him.

The love that resulted in Jesus laying aside all the beauty and perfection of heaven, to share in the limitations of human life, and then to be killed without cause by sinful people, is so great that he rightly deserves all our energy and devotion.

To think about *'Love so amazing, so divine, demands*

BIBLE CHECK
Called by God: Romans 6:15–19; Ephesians 2:8–10
Compelled by love: John 13:34,35; Romans 5:3–5;

my soul, my life, my all'. Discuss the implications of these lines from Isaac Watts' hymn.

Committed through faith

Part of being a Christian is a willingness to do whatever God wants.

He wants to change our lives so that we become more like Jesus. For this to happen we need to accept his instructions and rebukes.

Since we are already committed to letting him work in our lives, he now wants us to follow his instructions one step further, and commit ourselves to serving him in the world.

To think about *What are some of the common objections which people raise to excuse themselves from serving Jesus in the world? How should we answer them?*

Concerned for others

There are many people in every community who have physical or spiritual needs. Some of them may need help just to live more comfortably – people such as the poor and disabled.

Others are lonely and need human friendship; most probably the majority of them still need to find Jesus as their Saviour and friend.

It is easy for us to be so concerned with ourselves that we are blind to the needs of others. But God wants us to grow more sensitive to other people's needs, and to help them whenever we can.

To think about *Why did Jesus help so many needy people? What does that teach us about our responsibilities?*

Postscript *There are many things which we could do for God, so we need to pray for his guidance to know exactly what tasks he has for us to do.*

---

2 Corinthians 5:14,15
Committed through faith: Matthew 24:45–47; Romans 12:1,2
Concerned for others: Matthew 9:36; 14:14; 1 Peter 3:8

BIBLE SUMMARY

Pictures of service

The New Testament writers use a number of pictures to describe God's people as they seek to serve him. Here are a few of them.

Employed on God's business

A frequent description is that of a slave, or servant. In Bible times, slaves were common in society. They worked for one man, and while some of them had a great deal of personal freedom, they were 'bound' to their master – they could not leave his service.

Paul regarded himself as the slave of Jesus (Romans 1:1; 1 Timothy 1:12), and said that all Christians were to live as if they were the slaves of God (Ephesians 6:6). Another similar description he uses is that of 'stewards', who were managers of houses and estates, and who were required to be honest and faithful to their employer (1 Corinthians 4:1,2).

Working for God's kingdom

Paul sometimes thought of himself as a builder, laying the foundations of faith in Jesus (1 Corinthians 3:10–15), or as a farmer who plants seed (the word of God) which others tend and help grow to maturity (1 Corinthians 3:5–9).

He thought of himself as a soldier, too, fighting both to defend the truth and to defeat evil by bringing others into God's kingdom (1 Timothy 6:12; 2 Timothy 4:7).

Following Jesus' footsteps

Perhaps the most helpful picture is of a 'disciple', one who follows in his master's footsteps, always willing to learn and to obey. Jesus' disciples were his pupils and fellow-workers (e.g. Luke 8:9,10; 9:1–6; 11:1).

To think and pray about *Which pictures apply to you? How can you become more useful in your service for Jesus?*

A CROSS ABOVE ZERMATT (Adrian Neilson)
Mark's Gospel constantly reveals Jesus in active service for others, summarised in the famous statement of Jesus, 'The Son of Man did not come to be served, but to serve, and to give his life as a ransom for many.'

POWER TO SERVE

The key truth *It is possible to do God's work in God's way only by relying entirely on the power given to us by his Holy Spirit.*

Sharing God's work

Christians are called to share in the work God has been doing, and will continue to do, in the world. It is *his* continuing work, not ours.

That does not mean we can lay aside the skills and knowledge we have gained in the world. But it is easy to assume that God must approve anything we do in connection with telling others about Jesus, or helping in the life of the church. In fact, we can only be sure of what is his work by regularly seeking his guidance. Sometimes, things are done in churches only because they have always been done.

To think about *What tests would you apply to an idea, to find out if it really was part of God's work?*

Filled with his Spirit

Whenever the first Christians set out on a new venture, they asked for God's Spirit to fill their lives with the power and wisdom they needed to do his work.

And as they went out in faith, they often discovered that God had already gone ahead, preparing people to receive their message.

When we take part in God's work, we need to do it in his way, and not depend merely on human ideas and methods. Only as we allow the Holy Spirit to flow through us will we see the results of God's love working in our community or church.

To think about *How can we keep open to God's Spirit?*

BIBLE CHECK

Sharing God's work: John 14:12–14; 2 Corinthians 6:1
Filled with his Spirit: Acts 8:26–30; 13:1–4; Ephesians 5:18

Controlled by his Word

God does not want us to go into the world to teach our own ideas about him. He has given us his Word – the truth of his nature and our needs – to proclaim and to live out.

That Word carries the authority of God himself. However people react to us and our message, we need never doubt its truth and relevance. The living God has stamped it with his power.

However, we are not to become like parrots, repeating key phrases in answer to every question, as some non-Christian sects teach their members. God's Word is big and powerful enough to be explained and applied in ways which make sense in our society without losing its truth and authority.

To think about *Why does it make sense to let God's Word direct every aspect of our life?*

Equipped with his gifts

Jesus told a story about a man who gave his servants money – the coinage was called 'talents' – to use for the man's profit while he was away on business.

All except one were faithful, and made use of their gifts with varying degrees of success. All were praised, except for the servant who buried his gift in the sand.

God has given us personal abilities to use for him. There are natural talents he gave us when we were born, and there are spiritual gifts he wants us to seek, too. We always have the resources to do whatever he calls us to.

To think about *Why do you think the servant in Jesus' story refused to use his talent? What can we learn from that?*

Postscript *Christian service is as much an act of faith as anything else in the Christian life. We are not called to be timid, but faithful and bold, trusting in God's power.*

Controlled by his Word: John 17:14; Acts 4:31; 1 Corinthians 2:1–5
Equipped with his gifts: Matthew 25:14–30; Ephesians 4:7

BIBLE SUMMARY

Doing what comes naturally

The church is sometimes pictured by Paul as a body. Each person has a particular job to do, just as each part of the human body has its own function.

Working together

So, says Paul, chaos would rule if the foot thought itself useless because it was not a hand, or if the head told the feet that they were not needed (1 Corinthians 12:14–21).

In fact, he goes on, God has given the apparently weaker parts of both the human body and 'the body of Christ' an indispensable role (vs. 22–26). The Bible gives no justification for creating in Christian service a hierarchy of jobs according to the power or status they are thought to carry. We have one master, Jesus, and all are called to serve him (Matthew 23:8–12).

Being ourselves

Everyone likes to be thought well of by others, and respected for their abilities. Christians are to respect one another for what each has to offer, recognising that all have something of value to give (see Philippians 2:3,4).

Therefore we can be free to do whatever God wants – whether it is leading a church or counting the money, speaking at meetings or providing refreshments – without feeling at all inferior or superior.

And that means the hypocrisy which Jesus so strongly condemned need never appear in our churches (see, for example, Matthew 23:1–7, 13–15, 23–28). Then, God is free to do just what he wants through us – which is always a great deal!

To think and pray about *Why is it often hard to be simple, natural and honest?*

SHARING AND CARING (Robert G. Hunt)
There are all kinds of ways in which we can 'serve' both within the church, and in society. Of supreme importance is that whatever we do we should do it joyfully 'as working for the Lord'.

SERVING IN THE CHURCH

The key truth *There are as many things to do for one another in the church as there are members of it.*

The first shall be last

When two of Jesus' twelve apostles came to him to ask for the best seats in heaven, the rest of the group were naturally upset.

Jesus took the opportunity to explain to them all that, in his kingdom, the greatest person was in fact the one who was slave to the rest. In other words, service to God is more important than the praise of men.

Jesus taught that the really great people are often those who are despised by others because they are humble rather than ruthless or ambitious, or because they are not very fortunate or gifted.

To think about *Why do you think there is such a marked difference between the Christian and non-Christian attitudes to rank and respect?*

Lending a hand

Some churches probably have too much organisation – too many committees and planning meetings and administrative tasks. Such things can easily get in the way of our calling to teach and live out the simple message of God's love.

But every church must have some organisation, because God wants us to reflect his character, which brings order out of chaos.

There are all kinds of things which need doing today, just as there were in the early church. Everyone can help with cleaning or making things, looking after buildings or children, and arranging activities or meetings.

To think about *How can you find out what needs doing in your church?*

BIBLE CHECK
The first shall be last: Mark 9:35–45; Matthew 19:29,30
Lending a hand: Acts 6:1–3; Romans 12:7,8,13

Caring for the needy

Love, expressed by caring for the poor, the ill, the disabled, the sorrowful, the weak and the homeless has always been a characteristic of the Christian church.

There are people in every congregation who have needs which others can meet. They may require help to buy food or keep their homes tidy. They may be lonely, sad or afraid, and need the comfort and security of someone else's friendship.

Sometimes, this care demands special skills of counselling, to help people apply Jesus' truth to their deepest needs. But often it is just a matter of being available to others to let the love of Jesus flow through us.

To think about *What are the greatest needs of individuals in your church?*

Speaking God's word

This is often, and wrongly, regarded as the most important aspect of Christian service. It is important, but should not be allowed to overshadow other aspects.

There are many ways we can speak God's word. Some will have opportunities to teach or preach at meetings. Others will be able to contribute to discussions. A few may be given, by the Spirit, God's special word of encouragement or warning to the church, which others must test by the scriptures.

But there are also gifts of singing, writing, acting, dancing, painting and so on; which can all speak God's word in some way. And above all, so too can our daily conversations with friends, neighbours and work colleagues.

To think about *What qualifications does someone need before he can speak the word of God to others?*

Postscript *Just as each person has something to give, so we also each have something to receive. Christian service is mutual; we must be as willing to be helped as we are to help.*

Caring for the needy: 1 Thessalonians 5:14; James 2:14–17
Speaking God's word: 1 Corinthians 14:3–5,29–32; 1 Timothy 4:1–5

BIBLE SUMMARY

Building community

God intended that all human beings should live in a community of giving and receiving, and of mutual sharing; it is not possible to live a fully human life alone (Genesis 2:18).

The world has long since become a very selfish place, in which everyone fends for himself, and rarely helps others at his own expense (Luke 11:37–42; 16:19–31).

The church, however, is meant to be the place where God's new community, his kingdom, is made visible to the world as an example of true love and care (see 1 Peter 2:9,10).

Growing together

This ideal can only be reached as Christians learn to share their lives together as fully as possible. That involves more than meeting together regularly, important as that is (Hebrews 10:23–25).

In addition, we need to get to know one another in such a way that we can function like a fit and mature body, without limping or stumbling (1 Corinthians 12:25–27). To achieve this our church life will become much more than a pastime; it will be the centre of our life.

To think and pray about *What are the basic ways in which we can contribute to the building of a true Christian community?*

A COMMUNITY OF BEES (Alan Hayward)
The Christian fellowship is God's community, where his presence, holiness and greatness can be appreciated; where his mercy and grace can be experienced, and through which his light and love can be demonstrated.

INTO THE WORLD

The key truth *God wants his people to show through their behaviour, speech and church life the difference Jesus has made to them.*

A life that is different

A Christian is a human being like everyone else. That means we all share the same emotional, spiritual and physical needs. If we pretend to be above these needs, we shall appear cold and inhuman – something Jesus never was.

But at the same time we *are* different. God's Spirit is active in our lives. We belong to God's kingdom, which has a different set of values from our human society.

The Christian life is based on love for God and our neighbour. This is meant to result in caring deeply for others, and in avoiding all kinds of sin. We will not need to be like the Pharisees in Jesus' day who tried to impress people by their good deeds. People will simply see Jesus in us.

To think about *Read the passage from Ephesians 5. List the characteristics of the Christian life which Paul gives and discuss how they can be applied.*

Lips that are pure

It is always much easier to speak harshly than kindly. And it is easier to curse than to bless, to lie than to tell the truth.

But all these easier things spring from our selfish nature and not from God. We are his representatives in the world, so our conversation should reflect his attitudes. This means that swearing, boasting, lying (even small, 'white' lies) and impatient anger are out. Rather, he wants us to be loving, gracious, truthful and patient.

BIBLE CHECK
A life that is different: Matthew 6:1–14; Ephesians 5:3–20
Lips that are pure: Ephesians 4:25–32; 1 Peter 3:8–12

To think about *How may we learn to control our speech?*

Little things count

There is a false idea that the only things that really count for God are the big, important actions and decisions.

That is the devil's own lie; with God little things are extremely important. Only when we are faithful to him in them can we hope to be faithful in larger issues.

So Jesus and his followers said that the little actions of love, and seemingly unimportant words of help or encouragement, are vital. They are ways of showing God's care for the details of life.

To think about *For Thy sake:*
'A servant with this clause, makes drudgery divine:
Who sweeps a room, as for Thy laws,
Makes that and the action fine.'
What does George Herbert's verse say to us today?

Loving our enemies

Christian love is demanding and far-reaching. Jesus said that most people love those who are kind to them, but that his followers were to love their enemies as well.

This kind of love was to take two forms. There was 'going the second mile' – doing more for people than they insisted on. And there was the attitude of being kind and forgiving towards those who insulted or persecuted Christians. Jesus showed us an example of that by praying for the forgiveness of those who were nailing him to the cross.

To think about *Why do you think Jesus gave us such a difficult instruction? How can we carry it out?*

Postscript *The Christian life does not consist simply of following set patterns of conduct; God wants our total lifestyle to reflect his character so that the world may truly recognise him.*

Little things that count: Matthew 10:40–42; Colossians 3:17
Loving our enemies: Matthew 5:38–48; 26:48–54; Luke 23:34

BIBLE SUMMARY

Pilgrims in a strange land

Every Christian is a member of God's kingdom. The rest of the world is not. We are, therefore, in this life like 'strangers and pilgrims' in a foreign land. Our way of life reflects the love and laws of God (see 1 Peter 2:11,12).

Residents of the world

We are not told to form our own separate communities quite cut off from the rest of the world (John 17:15; 1 Corinthians 5:9–13). That would be almost impossible, and would restrict our witness for God.

Christians are encouraged in the Bible to observe the laws of the land and to pay their taxes, always bearing in mind that they cannot obey a law which prevents them doing what God commands, or orders them to do something wrong. (See Jesus' example in Matthew 17:24–27; his teaching in Matthew 22:15–22, and in the apostles' application of it in Romans 13:1–7; 1 Peter 2:13–17).

Citizens of heaven

Despite this Jesus reminds us that we are not of the world (John 17:16) – our citizenship is now in heaven (Philippians 3:20). Therefore we are God's 'ambassadors' on earth (2 Corinthians 5:20), living out our new life in a sometimes hostile environment among people who do not know God. But at the same time, we are to tell them about him.

To think and pray about *Discuss situations when you might have to disobey human laws in order to keep God's.*

TRACKS IN A GHOST TOWN, CALICO, USA
(Robert F. Hicks)
As Christians we need not be ashamed, discouraged or feel cheated because we are called to be pilgrims. All that the world is and has to offer will pass away, because it belongs to the past, not the future.

SHARING GOOD NEWS

The key truth *Jesus has told his people to take his message of new, eternal life and forgiveness to the whole world.*

A message for everyone

There is no message the world needs to hear more than the message of Jesus. Everyone needs to hear about him. Their only certain hope of enjoying his love now and for ever is to trust him, just as we have done.

No one is too old, young, clever or illiterate to be able to know Jesus for themselves. His death on the cross was for everyone who would accept it.

So important is the 'gospel', the good news, that one of the last things Jesus told his followers was to travel everywhere to proclaim it.

To think about *What do these Bible passages tell us about the relationship to God of people of other faiths?*

Talking about Jesus

After the first wave of persecution in the early church, the followers of Jesus scattered across several countries. Wherever they went, they told people about Jesus.

In some ways it is natural to tell people about things that mean a lot to us – special events which have happened, new people we have met. So it should be natural to tell them about Jesus and what he has done for us.

Some Christians find it hard to put their faith into words, because it is a deeply personal thing. But there is usually something we can say, at the right moment; a comment, perhaps, about how Jesus promises to deal with some difficulty people are talking about, or just a verse from the Bible which is relevant to a conversation.

To think about *Read the story in Acts 9; Ananias is an otherwise unknown disciple. Discuss how he must have felt*

BIBLE CHECK
A message for everyone: Matthew 28:18–20; John 3:16,17; Acts 4:11,12

when told to go and tell the notorious persecutor of Christians about Jesus' love.

Letting God work

There is 'a time to be silent and a time to speak', advises a wise Old Testament writer. While most of us probably do not speak enough about Jesus, sometimes we may choose the wrong moment or manner.

God uses our words, but sometimes we need to be patient, and let his word, through his Spirit, work in someone's mind or heart.

God has gifted certain people in telling others about Jesus and leading them to him. They need our prayers and financial support. We may just be able to interest someone enough to encourage them to meet or hear an evangelist.

To think about *What is the relationship between our activity and that of the Holy Spirit in spreading the gospel?*

Telling the neighbourhood

Paul, in the New Testament, is well known for his missionary strategy. He did not work without a plan. He went to the important places and people to proclaim Jesus, leaving behind him a group of Christians who would be able to tell others in their district and beyond.

His example is a good one to follow. There may be groups of people in an area who will be specially open to the gospel. Or there may be areas where there is no witness, to which we could reach out.

The work of evangelism – telling the good news – is something we can all share in, by our own personal witness, by delivering leaflets, visiting others' homes, helping with special church services, and so on.

To think about *What can you do to help spread the gospel in your area?*

Postscript *It is easy to be discouraged by a lack of response to our efforts, and so concentrate on our church fellowship. But Jesus calls us to keep on proclaiming him, with the methods which are most appropriate in our area.*

Talking about Jesus: Acts 8:4–8; 9:10–19
Letting God work: Ecclesiastes 3:7; John 12:20–23; Luke 1:76–79; 3:4
Telling the neighbourhood: Acts 17:16–18; 18:1–4

BIBLE SUMMARY

All things to all men

Paul told the Corinthians that in his task of proclaiming the good news of Jesus, he became 'all things to all men' (1 Corinthians 9:22). The phrase is sometimes used to describe people who are unreliable, just as a chameleon changes the colour of its skin to blend in with its surroundings; they adapt their words or actions so they will always be accepted.

Identifying with people

That, however, was not Paul's meaning. Rather, he did all he could to identify closely with the people he went to, so that he did not make his message sound like something totally irrelevant to their needs or culture.

So to the Jews, he proclaimed Jesus in the context of being the 'king of the Jews', the promised Messiah (v.20). To non-Jews, he emphasised the fact that Jesus came to save the whole world, and that God is not concerned with racial differences (v.21).

To people in personal need, Paul preached the tenderness and care of Jesus, which he himself knew and experienced (v.22). His reason was not to change the message, but to adapt the way he taught it to the needs of the moment.

Jesus own example

In doing this, he was following Jesus' own example. His favourite name for himself was 'Son of Man' (e.g. Luke 5:24), through which he closely identified with us.

He, too, adapted his methods. He used parables to some people and direct teaching to others (Matthew 13:10–18), for example.

To think and pray about *What methods for proclaiming the gospel would be most appropriate in your area?*

JAPANESE IN A TRADITIONAL DRESS

(Robert G. Hunt)

Some aspects of all cultures are alien to God, but the gospel of Jesus Christ enriches all that is good.

SERVICE FOR LIFE

The key truth *Every Christian is in full-time service for Jesus; there are not part-timers or reservists in God's 'army'.*

Ready for change

The Holy Spirit is dynamic – he is always on the move, always working. We, on the other hand, usually prefer a quiet life which is secure and stable.

When Jesus spoke to the church in Ephesus, he said that while they had been faithful to him, they had lost their first love. They needed to be open to change, ready to follow him wherever he led, just as they had once done.

That has always been a challenge to Christians. We need to ask frequently, 'Lord, what do you want me to do?'

To think about *Discuss the ways in which the Holy Spirit seems to be doing new things in your area or experience, and the ways you can share in it.*

Giving everything to Jesus

In one sense, we have already given everything to Jesus – our whole selves, our lives, in return for his forgiveness and new life.

But there may be a further way in which he wants us to give ourselves to him; by being willing to give up our jobs and join the staff of a church or missionary society, or enter some other form of Christian work.

Our commitment to him may also be expressed in our willingness to give up more of our spare time to take on church responsibilities. However, if we have families, it is important not to neglect them.

To think about *What are the essential qualifications for someone to serve God in Christian work?*

BIBLE CHECK
Ready for change: Revelation 2:1–7; John 3:8
Giving everything to Jesus: Jeremiah 1:4–10; Luke

Supporting his workers

'The worker deserves his wages' is a New Testament principle which reminds us that church leaders and workers, some of whom have given up well-paid jobs to serve Jesus in the church, need food to eat and clothes to wear.

And if we do not provide those things for them, they will be hungry and cold. God expects us to share their ministry to us by sharing our earnings and goods with them.

Paul considered that such support was a right. In Corinth, however, he did not exercise that right, to avoid being a burden on the church. Instead, he earned money by making tents. But that was his personal decision, and did not alter the principle on which he usually worked.

To think about *How does your church support its staff? What are you also able to do to support workers who have gone from your area to other places?*

Praying for God's servants

Some people do not seem to have much to give in the way of Christian service. They may be old or infirm, poor, or with little time to give to the church.

But of course, they can love and care about others. And above all, like everyone else, they can give time to prayer.

God works the world over through the prayers of his people. Moses, the Jewish leader, once needed someone to support him physically as he led Israel in battle; through prayer, we support spiritually those who are on the front line of spiritual warfare. Without us, the going could be tougher.

To think about *How can you put prayer back to its prime position in Christian service?*

Postscript *Christian service is a work of love. It is hard work, and it is more effective when it stems from our love for Jesus and his people.*

10:1–12; Romans 10:14–17
Supporting his workers: Luke 10:7; 1 Corinthians 9:3–18
Praying for God's servants: Exodus 17:10–13; Colossians 1:9; 4:2–4

BIBLE SUMMARY

Paul, a servant of God

In some respects Paul the apostle was an exceptional person. The amount of work he got through would have killed a lesser man (2 Corinthians 11:23–29)! But despite that, his service for Jesus remains an inspiring model for us to follow.

Dedicated to Jesus

Paul did not believe in doing things by halves. Jesus had given everything for him, so he gave everything for Jesus (Galatians 2:20).

Such was his dedication that he never slackened off right up to his death (2 Timothy 4:6–8). That is the basis of all Christian service; we cannot expect to achieve great things for God unless we are ready to follow him fully.

Controlled by God's word

Before his conversion Paul was a Jewish scholar (Galatians 1:14) with a good knowledge of the Old Testament scriptures. After his conversion, God revealed the full truth about Jesus to him (Galatians 1:11,12), which was in full agreement with what the other apostles had been teaching (Galatians 2:1,2).

All his teaching was firmly built on the basic facts of who Jesus was and what he had done on the cross, and Paul firmly resisted all attempts to alter that gospel or add to it (Galatians 1:6–9; 2 Timothy 1:11–14). That is a key to effective Christian service; we cannot expect to win others for Jesus or to help other Christians to grow, if we are not firmly teaching and applying his truth.

To think and pray about *Perhaps Paul was exceptional only because few other people have had the same degree of dedication. What do you think?*

Arriving

The hope that we have in Christ is not a 'may be' but a certainty. Jesus himself has gone to prepare a place for us, so that we might be with him eternally.

As we look forward to that great day of fulfilment of the promises in Christ for us we should be . . .

Living that life now

Facing grief or death with hope

Recognising that accountability is unavoidable

Recognising that perfection is guaranteed

Recognising that 'new beginnings' will take place.

'We know that when he appears, we shall be like him, for we shall see him as he is. Everyone who has this hope in him purifies himself, just as he is pure' (1 John 3:2,3).

TOP OF THE MATTERHORN (Adrian Neilson)

ON THE ROAD TO HEAVEN

The key truth *The Christian always has heaven in his sights.*

Heaven on earth

Every person who has recognised that Jesus Christ's death on the cross was God's way of offering forgiveness and eternal life and who has personally asked for that forgiveness and life, will without a doubt go to heaven when he dies.

For us, eternal life has already begun; God's love has broken into our earthly life. His Holy Spirit has started the process of turning our sinful nature into something pure and perfect which will be completed in heaven.

And the Spirit brings the life of heaven to us by giving us both confidence (or assurance) that we belong to Jesus and his power to overcome sin and evil. Sometimes, too, in our prayers we will become specially conscious that we are no longer bound to earth but are bound for heaven.

To think about *In what ways can our spiritual or eternal life be seen and known in our daily experience?*

Life in perspective

Most people live as if this life were all that mattered. They spend lots of energy and time gathering possessions or working to achieve some status or recognition in the world.

But Jesus taught that life on earth is important, precisely because it is the period of time we have been given to come to terms with God's purposes for us.

Those purposes embrace the whole world and the whole of eternity. That gives our life now a small but still very significant place in his plans. And it puts a comparatively short earthly life into a new perspective: eternity never ends!

BIBLE CHECK

Heaven on earth: Ephesians 3:14–21; Titus 3:3–7

To think about *Try to imagine your life in the context of eternity – or even just in the context of world history. How does that help you come to terms with the problems you currently face?*

Aiming for goal

We all need an aim in life, otherwise we drift about and are never satisfied. The aim of the Christian life is to please Jesus.

But there is also another goal to aim for, which we cannot miss, but which should determine how we go about pleasing him.

That goal is to spend eternity in his presence. If that is where we are going, then every thought, word and deed in this life deserves to be worthy of his presence.
To think about *How can we apply to ourselves Paul's comments about personal discipline in 1 Corinthians 9?*

Ready for Jesus

Human nature is the same all over the world. Jesus was aware that Christians could be as lazy as anyone else. So several of his parables about the end of time showed how we should live now in readiness for the next life.

In one story he showed how five girls did not bother to prepare themselves for a marriage festival, so that when it happened, they were not let in.

And in another, a servant decided to live selfishly and to hurt others, because his master was away and seemed delayed in returning home. He thought it would not matter, but he was punished. Jesus said, 'You must be ready, for you do not know when the Son of Man is 'coming.'
To think about *What practical effect is being ready for Jesus likely to have on our life?*

Postscript *There are two uncertainties in life: one is the time of our death, the other is the time of Jesus' return to earth. The Bible tells us to be ready for both.*

Life in perspective: Luke 9:24,25; 16:19–31
Aiming for goal: 1 Corinthians 9:24–27; Philippians 3:8–17
Ready for Jesus: Matthew 24:45–25:13

BIBLE SUMMARY

Hope springs eternal

When hope dies, life becomes almost impossible (Job 19:10). Everyone needs something to look forward to, to work for, to spur them on. Whether the Christian life for us is very hard or comparatively trouble-free, the hope of eternal life with Jesus is said in the New Testament to be the spur we need in order to be faithful to him, who is faithful to us.

Hope in God's promises

Hope is closely linked to faith in the Bible (e.g. 1 Corinthians 13:13). Hope like faith is confidence that God will fulfil his promises. 'Against all hope, Abraham in hope believed' that God would make him, a childless husband, the ancestor of many nations (Romans 4:18–21). Similarly, when we are experiencing difficulty or testing, hope is strengthened as we endure suffering by the power of God: we see what he can do, and his love gives hope that he will continue to sustain us (Romans 5:1–5).

Hope in God's provision

Most of all, hope is something the New Testament writers link to eternal life (Titus 1:2). Hope is the basis of our faith in Jesus (Ephesians 1:18–20; 1 Peter 1:3); we look forward to what God has prepared for us in heaven, which is far better than the best things the world has to offer. Therefore, our life now can be one of self-sacrifice (Colossians 1:4,5), because our hope outweighs any inconvenience we may experience. We cannot see our hoped-for home with Jesus (Romans 8:24,25), but we wait for it patiently, while Jesus' life within us fuels that hope and keeps it alive (Colossians 1:27).

To think and pray about *Put in your own words what is special about the hope we have.*

ANCHOR CHAINS, QUEEN MARY, LONG BEACH, CAL., USA (Robert F. Hicks)
Hope takes hold of the future, heaven and God's promises, as well as giving stability to our lives as the anchor of our souls.

COPING WITH BEREAVEMENT

The key truth *Jesus brings a new perspective of hope to the sad experience of bereavement.*

Coping with our grief

'Jesus wept': that is the shortest verse in the Bible. But the words sum up the deep feelings of Jesus at the tomb of one of his closest friends, Lazarus.

The customs of showing grief in public vary from country to country, but the feelings of grief are very natural and it is not weak or un-Christian to mourn the death of those we love. After all, they have given much to us, for which we are deeply grateful.

But Christians need not grieve 'like the rest of men, who have no hope'. Sad as is the loss to us personally, we can also rejoice that a believing person has gone to be with the Lord for ever. Yet the loss of unsaved loved ones is an agony beyond words.

To think about *Discuss how the mixture of joy and sadness might affect a Christian funeral service.*

Coping with our loss

A time of bereavement is a time of conflicting emotions. The bereaved person wants to be alone, yet he also wants the company of friends.

It can easily turn into a time of bitterness when we complain that God has robbed us of someone we love. But of course, our loss means their blessing in his presence.

His perfect plan has allowed for the right time of death for each person, hard as that may sometimes be to understand. One day those who belong to Christ will be reunited; meanwhile, we have the loving presence of Jesus.

BIBLE CHECK
Coping with our grief: John 11:28–37; 1 Thessalonians 4:13–18

To think about *How can we prepare ourselves for the loss of people we love?*

Coping, with Jesus' help

Because Jesus has experienced both bereavement and death itself, he knows how to comfort those who mourn.

He always showed deep concern and sympathy with the bereaved. Because he never changes, he offers his peace to the troubled, his joy to the sorrowful, and his presence to the lonely.

That does not mean we will suffer no pain at all. But it does mean that because he has kept us here in this life for a little longer, he still has something useful for us to do.

To think about *How would you encourage someone who mourned to take the help Jesus offers?*

Helping others to cope

In New Testament times, the church always had a special place for widows. This was partly because there was always a welcome for the lonely, but mainly because without husbands they would become very poor.

So the church organised collections to help them pay for food, clothes and shelter. There are always things which the bereaved need help with, even in countries where they are not short of money.

Most of all, they need fellowship – the deep caring and sharing of Christians who are able to love and grieve together, and offer human spiritual support.

To think about *What practical help are the bereaved likely to need in your area?*

Postscript *An important element in coping with bereavement is being prepared to surrender those we love to Jesus, just as we have surrendered ourselves.*

Coping with our loss: 2 Corinthians 5:1–8; Revelation 7:9
Coping, with Jesus' help: Lamentations 3:19–33; Luke 7:12,13; John 14:27
Helping others to cope: 1 Timothy 5:3–16; James 1:27

BIBLE SUMMARY

Why must we die?
Death is unpleasant, sometimes painful, and always sad. And that in itself partly answers the question as to why it happens. Death is a result of the imperfection and fallenness of mankind (Genesis 3:19; 1 Corinthians 15:56).

No exceptions
Because we all share in the sinfulness of the world, we all have to die (Ezekiel 18:4; Romans 6:23). Death has been called the great leveller; the best and the worst people all have to go through it.

The Bible records only a couple of instances of 'translation' – the sudden transformation from this life to the next without death. One was Enoch (Genesis 5:24; Hebrews 11:5) and the other Elijah, who was seen being taken into heaven in a whirlwind (2 Kings 2:11).

The only other exceptions will be when Jesus returns to earth. Christians who are alive then will be taken straight to heaven (1 Corinthians 15:51,52; 1 Thessalonians 4:17).

Death defeated
Death is no longer the unconquerable enemy it once was. Jesus has defeated it by dying and being raised to life. While we must still experience death, a continued life with Jesus is waiting beyond it for all who have accepted his death as God's way of dealing with their sins (See Romans 5:12–21).

To think and pray about *Why do you think God did not abolish death immediately after Jesus rose from the dead?*

CROCUSES IN SPRING (Alan Hayward)
Each year we witness 'new life' all around us, yet in spite of this annual reminder through nature man still prefers to reject life after death. As Christians we not only believe in but, in part, experience that resurrection life in Christ now.

FACING DEATH

The key truth *Because of Jesus' death and resurrection, we can face our own death with confidence rather than fear.*

Life completed

There is no guarantee that a person will live for a certain length of time. Sometimes people die from disease, accident or violence long before we think they should.

That is part of the tragedy of a sinful world. Some people do not have the opportunity to do all they could usefully accomplish. Therefore, we always need to be ready to return to God who made us.

But he alone knows how useful we really are, and his purposes will never be defeated by premature death. When he calls us to be with him for ever, we know that we will have done our part for him on earth.

To think about *Why does our estimate of a person's usefulness so often differ from God's estimate?*

Saying goodbye

Our attitude to death will depend very much on our attitude to life – which is as good a reason as any to prepare ourselves for it.

If we have been largely selfish, allowing ourselves to be dominated by possessions, wealth, privileges and human status, it will be very hard to let go of these things as death approaches.

But if our life has been characterised by giving, sharing and loving, then it will not be so hard to say goodbye. We can be sure that the Lord who will look after us in eternity will also look after the people we leave behind.

To think about *Discuss how we can adopt an attitude to*

BIBLE CHECK
Life completed: Philippians 1:19–26; 2 Timothy 4:6–8
Saying goodbye: Job 1:21; Psalm 68:5,6; Mark 10:17–31

our possessions which is willing to release them before or at death.

A place for repentance

Sometimes, when death approaches, people are very conscious of all the wrong things they have done in their life. They remember the hasty words, the unkind actions, the forgotten promises and neglected duties. While it is never too late to repent and be saved or experience restored relationships with God or others we have wronged, it is sad to learn so late the joy that reconciliation brings.

The aim for every Christian should be to confess each sin as it happens all through life, in order to keep close to Jesus and experience his love and help.

To think about *How would you answer someone who says they will leave their repentance until the last possible moment?*

The doorway to heaven

Death, for the Christian, is not the end of life but, as it were, the gateway through which he passes to experience a new phase of the eternal life Jesus has given him.

Much of the fear of death arises because both it, and what lies beyond it, are largely unknown.

But Jesus has been through it – and come back again. The heaven he spoke of, and which was revealed to some Bible writers, is not a place to fear but to look forward to.

To think about *Why do you think the prospect of heaven is often neglected by Christians? What value is there in thinking about it?*

Postscript *Death, like life, is God's gift. The Bible does not allow us to take our own or anyone else's life even though we may, as believers, be certain of eternal life.*

A place for repentance: Psalm 103:1–14; Isaiah 53:1–12
The doorway to heaven: 1 Corinthians 15:3–19; Revelation 7:16,17

BIBLE SUMMARY

Life's last chance

Jesus once told a story about men who were employed to work in the fields. Some were hired in the morning, others at midday, and still others only a short while before dusk. Yet each received the same wages (Matthew 20:1–16).

The story was intended to show that it does not matter when a person becomes a Christian. All receive the same gift of eternal life, however much of their life has been spent working for Jesus. Christ made the point strongly when he promised that same gift to the thief who was crucified beside him, and who repented just before his death (Luke 23:39–43).

No second chances

However, it is in this life that we are called on to turn away from our sins and look to Jesus for eternal life. There is only one verse in the Bible which implies that those already dead may have a second chance, and it seems to apply only to those who lived in the years before Jesus came to earth (1 Peter 3:18–20).

Because the date of our death is uncertain, and because Jesus came into this world precisely to tell us the way to God in this life, the Bible message is always 'now is the day of salvation' (John 1:10–13; 3:14–18; 2 Corinthians 6:2).

To think and pray about *What does this truth tell us about our responsibility to proclaim the gospel?*

THE CLOCK, SANTA BARBARA, USA (Robert F. Hicks)

The time to accept Jesus as Saviour is always the present. This response must be accompanied by teaching, or explanation, so that the truth may be clearly understood.

ACTION REPLAY

The key truth *Every person who has ever lived will have their lives judged by God at the end of time.*

Nothing is hidden

Adam and Eve, you may remember, tried to do the impossible by hiding themselves from God. And Jesus once said that some religious leaders of his day were like whitewashed tombs – seemingly clean on the outside, but rotten inside.

What we really are, and what we really have done or not done, will be brought to light when the world is judged by God.

The Christian need not fear this judgement, because it cannot cost him his place in heaven – that is already secure. But it does remind us that we cannot abuse our gift of eternal life by living carelessly.

To think about *What can we do now about the things which may make us ashamed when God judges the world?*

The fire test

The major test for everyone is not how they have lived, because no one can enter heaven just because of the good things they have done. The question God will ask each one is, 'How did you treat my Son? Did you receive him or reject him?'

However, all Christians will have their lives assessed by God, to see how valuable they have been for him. Paul says some people's lives will be like wood, hay and stubble: they have done nothing worthwhile for God and his kingdom, and it will be as if their work just goes up in smoke.

Others' lives, however, will be like gold, silver and precious stones. They will survive the 'fire test' – the searching scrutiny of God's pure love and law – and will be built into the new heavens and earth.

BIBLE CHECK
Nothing is hidden: Luke 12:1–3; 2 Corinthians 5:6–15; Hebrews 9:27,28

To think about *Discuss the activities which could come under each heading: 'wood, hay, stubble' and 'gold, silver, precious stones'.*

Well done!

Christians will be spared detailed judgement which others will face. Instead, after their assessment mentioned above, they will be welcomed and praised by Jesus himself.

We cannot press the details of Jesus' parables too far, but in one of them God is pictured as giving his faithful servants degrees of responsibility in heaven, as a reward for their service on earth. Each reward exactly suits their abilities and achievements.

Paul also speaks of another reward – a 'crown', a symbol of victory and conquest over evil, which everyone will receive.

To think about *How important is the promise of God's rewards in heaven for our life here on earth?*

A place for you

Heaven is beyond imagination. Some people feel terrified at the thought of a huge mass of people all together; others cannot understand how we shall get on with each other!

But Jesus' promise to the individual is that there is a tailor-made place actually waiting for us to fill. He has gone ahead to get it ready for us.

One day, he is coming back to earth. Then, all Christians who have died will be raised from the dead, and they and the Christians still alive will be taken to be with Jesus.

To think about *What does the fact that there is a special place for us in heaven remind us about God's purposes for us on earth?*

Postscript *Although this part of our Christian life lies in the future, it will be no less real than our current experience. The Bible is full of predictions which have come true, and we can be confident these will, too.*

The fire test: 1 Corinthians 3:10–15; 1 John 4:16–19
Well done!: Matthew 25:14–30; 1 Corinthians 6:2,3; 2 Timothy 4:8
A place for you: John 14:1–7; 1 Thessalonians 4:16,17

BIBLE SUMMARY

The events of the end

The precise order of events surrounding Jesus' return to earth, and the end of the present world, is not entirely clear in scripture. This has led some people to do precisely what Jesus warned us against; attempting to predict the precise date, and speculate about certain events. (Matthew 24:4,36,44; 2 Thessalonians 2:1–4).

Short of grappling with the symbolism of Revelation, the best basic guide to 'the end' is Jesus' teaching in Matthew 24 (and the parallel passages in Mark 13:1–31 and Luke 21:1–33). Other teaching can then be fitted into that structure.

A time of suffering

The end days will be characterised by great suffering in the whole world (vs.6–8). This will be followed by intense persecution of Christians (vs.9–13), with false accusation, torture and murder. But the gospel still has to be preached in every part of the world before Jesus can return (v.14).

The 'abomination that causes desolation' (v.15) could relate to the anti-Christ spoken of by Paul (2 Thessalonians 2:3–12), a figure of great power who claims to be divine (see also v.24), but who is very evil.

Jesus takes over

After that 'great tribulation' the coming of Jesus will be seen by everyone (vs.27,30). He will come to judge the world, and demonstrate his great power in gathering to himself all his own people (v.31). Then he will create a new heaven and new earth, to be occupied only by those who have trusted him as their Saviour from sin and Lord of their life (Revelation 21:1).

To think and pray about *Why is speculation about the end so futile? How should we think about it?*

RED SKY AT NIGHT (Robert F. Hicks)
In Jesus' day, people were able to interpret the 'face of the sky' but not the 'signs of the times'. Christians must be careful about the way they apply biblical teaching about the future.

WELCOME HOME!

The key truth *Heaven is the Christian's final home, where we shall live for ever with Jesus and all his people.*

A place of peace

Heaven is a real place. Paul teaches that all Christians go straight to be with Jesus when they die, but that we do not take our final place in heaven until it is finally established at the end of the world.

But peace reigns as soon as we die. Our struggles are over. We are with Jesus in a closer, more personal way than we have ever experienced on earth.

In heaven, there are no wars. There are not even any arguments. And that is not because people have lost their personalities; it is because they have become perfectly human, as Jesus was when he lived on earth.

To think about *What promises can you recall which speak about peace in this life? How much do they foreshadow heaven?*

A place of joy

Heaven is a very joyful place. There is nothing there to be sad about!

But the joy is not a selfish kind of relief that evil and sin and suffering are a thing of the past. Rather it is rejoicing in the greatness, the glory and the love of God which fill heaven.

Worship will be a major activity. It will not simply be like an unending church service, though, but genuine praise from the hearts of people who have come to see more clearly the wonderful gift of eternal life given to them because of Jesus' death on the cross.

BIBLE CHECK

A place of peace: Compare Philippians 1:23 with 1 Thessalonians 4:17; Revelation 21:4–7

To think about *How can we make our worship on earth more like that of heaven?*

A place of beauty

Heaven is a brand new creation by God for his people. It will replace everything which existed before, although nothing which God originally made will be wasted.

It is therefore hard to imagine. Whenever the Bible writers describe it, they use picture language.

It is certainly a place of beauty and perfection – far better than anything which mankind has ever built. It is full of light and colour. Beyond that, we cannot imagine it – but no one will be disappointed by it!

To think about *Why has mankind never been able to build something as beautiful yet homely as God's new creation?*

A place of justice

Heaven is where justice will be seen to have been done. Everyone who truly belongs there will be there. And no one who has rejected Jesus and lived in selfishness and evil will be allowed to enter.

Then we shall see that wrongs have been put right – that will be part of our 'reward' – and that wrongdoers have received the punishment they deserved.

That state of peace, joy, beauty and justice will never end. No one can imagine what eternity really means, except that it makes our human life and all its concerns seem quite small.

To think about *What effect should this hope in God's justice have on our daily contact with other people?*

Postscript *People who believe in heaven are not excused from working to create peace, joy, beauty and justice on earth, where the first signs of God's kingdom are to be built.*

A place of joy: Revelation 4:8–11; 7:9–12
A place of beauty: Revelation 21:9–27; 22:1–5
A place of justice: Romans 12:17–21; Revelation 20:11–15; 21:8,27; 22:12–15

BIBLE SUMMARY

What happens to non-Christians
Despite the beauties and attractions of heaven, Jesus spent much time talking about the fate of those who rejected him. He did not paint a very pretty picture.

Excluded from God's presence
Jesus often used the picture of 'outer darkness' where there will be 'weeping and gnashing of teeth' (e.g. Matthew 24:30). It is a picture of people cut off for ever from the presence of God, from the warmth, love, peace and joy of heaven.

He also used the picture of an unquenched flame. It speaks of a place of frustration and unfulfilled desire, with people consuming themselves with anguish and sorrow. (See Mark 9:42–48; Luke 16:23,24,28; Revelation 20:14,15.)

The implication is that this state, usually called hell, lasts for ever. Certainly its *effect* is everlasting because there can be no transfers from it to heaven (Luke 16:26).

Jesus, the hope for the world
There is only one certain way of receiving eternal life, and that is to trust our lives entirely to Jesus Christ (John 14:6). That is why we are told to preach the gospel everywhere.

As for those who die without hearing about Jesus, Paul reminds us that God is always just and fair in his judgement of them (Romans 2:14–16). We cannot assume, however, that sinful men can attain that level of total faithfulness to what they have perceived of God's nature; hence the urgency of the missionary task.

To think and pray about *How would you talk to the bereaved relative of someone who was not a Christian?*

DRAMATIC SUNRISE OVER THE GRAND CANYON (Robert F. Hicks)
The dramatic and historic resurrection of Jesus Christ is the foundation of the Christian faith. Through the Holy Spirit it is more than that, being a daily experience in the life of the believer.

LIFE'S NEW BEGINNING

The key truth *The Christian's life has no end; death is the beginning of a new experience of life, love, peace and joy.*

All things new

'I am making everything new!' Those are some of the last recorded words of Jesus in the New Testament.

And 'everything new' means what it says: the physical earth, no longer corrupt and subject to decay; the organisations and systems which have controlled people's lives, no longer oppressive but creating order and freedom.

Everything which has existed will in some way be renewed and restored, for God wastes nothing. Only truly evil things will be totally destroyed. And this new creation depends as much on Jesus' death on the cross as our own eternal life does.

To think about *Why do you think God decided to 'reconcile to himself all things' rather than start everything again from scratch?*

A new body

When Jesus appeared to his closest followers after his death, he was usually recognisable. Some people even saw the marks of the nails which had fixed him to the cross. But his body was different, so that he seemed no longer bound to the earth by natural laws.

His resurrection body is the prototype of ours. The Bible says we will receive new bodies in heaven. Through them we shall express our true self; without them we would be frustrated spirits, like those in hell who do not receive new bodies.

It seems as though we shall recognise one another in heaven – but of course, all the old disabilities and infirmities will have been taken away.

BIBLE CHECK

All things new: Romans 8:19–23; Colossians 1:19–20; Revelation 21:5–7

To think about *What importance do you think we should place on what we look like in heaven? What does this imply for our present life?*

A new understanding

If you add up everything that is known in the world, it still only comes to a tiny proportion of what could be known. And each one of us only knows a tiny amount of the knowledge which does exist!

We are promised that when we get to heaven, we will understand much that has puzzled us on earth. However, even then we are not promised that we shall know everything – only God can be like that.

We may well understand some mysteries of our life – why God allowed this problem, or seemed not to answer that prayer – unless such issues are no longer of significance!

To think about *Why will some things remain a mystery to us until we reach heaven? How should we cope with them?*

A new kind of life

Heaven has often been wrongly pictured – usually by those who make fun of it. Some people think of it as an unending holiday, or an everlasting party.

In a sense it is, but that is only a part of the truth. The person who never wants to work will not be happy in heaven.

There will be lots to do, see, learn and experience. We will not cease to be human – in fact, we will have become truly human for the very first time. That means our life will be truly satisfying and stimulating – which a long period of idleness could never be. It is certainly something to look forward to!

To think about *What are you looking forward to most in heaven?*

Postscript *If Jesus is to make all things new in the future, he will not be content to leave us unchanged in the present; the change starts now.*

A new body: John 20:19–29; 1 Corinthians 15:35–54
A new understanding: 1 Corinthians 13:12; 1 Timothy 3:16; Revelation 7:13,14
A new kind of life: Matthew 22:1–13; Revelation 21:22–27